Monkey

ON A TURNTABLE

Monkey
ON A TURNTABLE

living on love
& leftovers in
local **radio**

by Ken Keller

ORANGE FRAZER PRESS
Wilmington, Ohio

ISBN 978-1-9331397-32-6

1-933197-32-3

The author's royalty from the sale of this book has been donated to the Kiwanis Club of
Columbus (Ohio) Scholarship Fund.

Additional copies of *Monkey on a Turntable* may be ordered directly from:

Orange Frazer Press

P.O. Box 214

Wilmington, OH 45177

Telephone 1.800.852.9332 for price and shipping information.

Website: www.orangefrazer.com

Cover design: Chad DeBoard

Book design: John Baskin and Chad DeBoard

Library of Congress Cataloging-in-Publication Data

Keller, Ken, 1939-

   Monkey on a turntable : living on love and leftovers in local radio

/ by Ken Keller.

        p. cm.

ISBN 978-1-933197-32-6 (alk. paper)

1. Keller, Ken, 1939- 2. Radio broadcasters--United States--Biography.

I. Title.

   PN1991.4.K43 2007

   791.4402'8'092--dc22

   [B]

                            2007016532

For Mary
... my one true *Ladylove*

Monkey on a Turntable

Chapter one
SIGN ON   2

Chapter two
REHEARSAL   10

Chapter three
SEX AFTER SIGN OFF   28

Chapter four
MONKEY ON A TURNTABLE   42

Chapter five
ART BECOMES LIFE... OR SOMETHING LIKE IT   58

Chapter six
THE MAN WHO (ALMOST) CAME TO DINNER   80

Chapter seven
A MESSAGE FROM GARCIA   100

Chapter eight
NOW ENTERING THE GAME   114

Chapter nine
THE WHITE PIANO   130

Chapter ten
SIGN OFF   144

Confessions & ACKNOWLEDGMENTS   156

Monkey
ON A TURNTABLE

THE AUTHOR, at 20, trying desperately not to look as callow as he is.

It had been snowing for several days. Not the snow of recent Columbus winters that largely melts on contact with roads and sidewalks, brewing first a soupy slush and later, after freezing, a moonscape of coarse, uneven ice. This was serious snow, the kind that makes curbs disappear without a trace and leaves a fire hydrant's snow-capped dome barely visible above a surrounding sea of white. When street lights reflecting from the frozen surface shatter into millions of tiny, crystalline stars, and a sound, any sound, travels forever without growing fainter.

The year, 1959, was brand new, and Ohio State University[1], my kingdom and my prison for most of the past seventeen months, had all but shut down in deference to the mounting drifts that clogged sidewalks and closed intersections. At the Phi Delta Theta house on Iuka Avenue, the brothers scoffed at the school's alarm but greedily anticipated that tomorrow's classes would be cancelled, automatically freeing them from any need to study that night. Some went off in search of an appropriate way to celebrate their pardon; I prepared to work my second shift of the day at WMNI Radio.

Since the preceding fall, I had been living my boyhood dream of becoming a radio broadcaster, with courses at Ohio State sandwiched in when time permitted. My parents would have preferred reversed priorities. Growing up in Toledo, Ohio, I had listened with fierce attention to network radio's Golden Age, absorbing countless hours of comedy, mystery, and drama that flowed from my bedroom radio in a river of words that still winds through my mind and memory.

I was on intimate terms with Don McNeill, Arthur Godfrey, Jack Benny, Bob Hope, The Great Gildersleeve, and Edgar Bergen and Charlie McCarthy, and I determined at a very early age to find where they lived and join them there.

My detour to Ohio State turned out to be no detour at all but rather a marvelous springboard into broadcasting. As a fraternity pledge, I was expected to identify some campus activity and become part of it. When I was slow to take this step, an active brother named Phil Brewer suggested that I accompany him to his extracurricular involvement: a student-staffed campus radio station that I will describe in more detail later. My experience with student radio was just sufficient to gain an audition at WMNI—then a brand new radio station in Columbus—and my willingness to work an impossible, part-time split shift for minimum wage sealed the deal.

There is one other player in this small drama that needs to be introduced before this chapter can proceed. During the preceding two summers I worked as a sheet metal and roofing laborer at The Fred Christen and Sons Company in Toledo. The company was founded by my mother's father and run then by three wonderful uncles who took delight in seeing one of their nephews endure the same trial-by-roofing-tar they remembered from their youths. With the money saved from this employment I had purchased my first car, a 1952 four-door Chevrolet.

Following family tradition I elected to personify my car, choosing for a name the current Broadway musical, *My Fair Lady*. It was, as it turned out, an ill-advised name, if by "fair" one means evenhanded, just, or equitable. MFL had proven as temperamental as a tenor and as prone to breakdown as Maria Callas.

In the short span of time I had been at Ohio State, the car had broken a timing chain, stranding me in Marion, Ohio, in the middle of the night at the center of a thunderstorm. It decided on another night to stop recharging its battery, causing the headlights and assorted other amenities to grow increasingly dim before shutting down altogether and depositing me on yet another unfamiliar berm. In addition, MFL often refused to recognize a perfectly good door key, leaving me hammering in loud and vulgar frustration on its solid gray roof.

Still, its newest peccadillo left me in open-mouthed wonder that any machine was capable of such evil. Once the temperature approached freezing, engaging the emergency brake was an invitation to remain where you were for the rest of the winter.

The brake shoes, once solidly in contact with the wheel drums, were very apt literally to freeze in that condition, preventing any forward movement of the car. Curiously, and for me inexplicably, the car would back up. It just refused to move forward so much as an inch.

There was one prescriptive solution to this dilemma, albeit a radical one. A mechanic had told me that you could open the trunk, rummage around for the jack and handle, jack the back end of the car as high as you could, and then, by pushing the car sideways off the jack, hope that the resulting crash would free the brake shoes from the drums. Astonishingly, it sometimes worked.

Now, as they used to say on radio, back to our story. It was 9:30 on this frosty winter's eve and time for me to leave the Phi Delt house for the drive downtown to go on the air at 10 and work the last hour of WMNI's broadcast day. For this service I would be paid an hour's minimum wage of one dollar.

The drive would normally take twelve to fifteen minutes, but I planned to leave early that evening in order to deposit my then-current Ladylove at her residence hall well before her 10:30 p.m., pull-out-your-fingernails-if-you're-late, curfew.

My Fair Lady was parked, as usual, adjacent to the fraternity house on a short but sharp incline. In order to have parked safely, setting the emergency brake was clearly the correct procedure. I, of course, knew better. Unfortunately, knowing better is not the same thing as remembering. Tumbling into the car, I backed successfully out of the parking space, down the incline, and into the street. It was only when I shifted into first and let out the clutch that my forgetfulness became instantly and horribly evident. MFL chugged once and stopped dead, as if a giant unseen hand held it fast to the pavement.

Experience told me that there was no use trying again for it intended to remain in the middle of the street until a snowplow, or spring, changed its wicked mind. Jumping out of the car, Ladylove bolted up the hill in search of help from a brother while I grabbed for the well-used jack and attempted the prescriptive solution. Once: crash! Twice: crash! A third time: crash! No use. The few additional minutes I had allotted for driving Ladylove to her dormitory had come and gone and I was still miles from where I needed to be.

OK, I thought. *Car will not go forward. Car will go backwards.* After all, I had just demonstrated as much backing down the drive. *If I can back a hundred feet, where is it written I can't back the four miles or so to the radio station?* No time to ponder consequences, I decided to give it a try.

Summoning Ladylove back into the car, we began inching up Iuka Avenue, around the traffic circle in front of the fraternity house, then down Waldeck to 16th Avenue. Turning right on 16th, then left on High, we arrived at its intersection with 15th, which was then the geographical and emotional heart of the campus.

Next we turned right on South Oval Drive. Oval Drive was "temporarily" closed to vehicular traffic during the campus riots of the Vietnam era and has remained so since.

The snow fell heavily on MFL's un-wipered rear window making forward visibility difficult. I opened my door with my left hand, steering with my right, and by shaping my body into a corkscrew, I was able to squint forward into the swirling flakes. Ladylove did the same on her side of the car. We backed past William Oxley Thompson Memorial Library and out onto Neil Avenue—not the most direct route downtown, but apt to be less traveled that night than High Street.

The street lamps on both sides of Neil Avenue created a tunnel of light in the darkness. Looking south as far as I could see there were no cars in motion, only mounds of snow bearing faint resemblance to automobiles lining both sides of the street. I was briefly troubled by which lane of traffic to choose: the right lane, appropriate for southbound cars, or the left lane, appropriate for north-facing traffic. I solved the dilemma by backing down the center of the street.

Eventually, the tall stone walls of the Ohio Penitentiary filled the rear window, and the half-light of street lamps and frantically churning snow filling spaces between its rough-cut stone blocks created a mood as Gothic as the structure itself. If O. Henry were still in residence at the prison, as he was for five years at the turn of the last century, I wondered what he would have written of our strange parade.

Past the penitentiary I backed left onto Spring Street and began climbing the gentle rise from the Scioto River into downtown. We'd been fortunate not to attract the attention of Columbus' finest, but two people hanging out the open doors of a car backing down the center of a street through a major state capital in a snowstorm might not go unnoticed forever.

The hour grew late, but so far I was still employed. I backed right onto High Street and passed the State Capitol where Lincoln once addressed the citizens of Columbus from its steps. A few more blocks and the great brick box of the Southern Hotel heaved into view. It was the Great Southern Fireproof Hotel when it was dedicated in 1896 and is the Columbus Westin Hotel as I write, following extensive and much-needed renovation, but in the mid-'50s it was just the Southern Hotel. WMNI's studios were in the penthouse. It was going to be close, but I thought I might just make it.

I compounded my other misdemeanors of the evening by parking MFL in a No Parking alley adjacent to the hotel, and my underage Ladylove in the Southern's lounge while I hammered repeatedly on the elevator controls, stupidly hoping to hurry the ancient cage on its descent. Eventually it appeared, I jumped in and began the pokey rise to the penthouse. Rushing breathless into the studio, I gasped out the call letters of the station at the 10 p.m. break, then allowed my weight to sag into the Play button on one of two temperamental tape recorders to begin a thirty minute prerecorded program that would see me halfway to sign-off. I fell into the chair at the console and hoped thirty minutes would be time enough to catch my breath.

The hands of the clock crept once around the dial, and at long last it was 11. I read the station sign-off, played the National Anthem, and turned out the lights. Racing to the elevator, I again hammered on the buttons, then paced back and forth as it dithered its way down to the lobby. Locating Ladylove in the lounge, I guided her unsteady footsteps out the door, pretending interest as she described the number and types of drinks that were purchased for her while she was waiting for me.

Please, God, let the car still be there. (It was.) *Please let it move forward when the clutch is let out.* (It didn't.) I threw open the trunk, ripped out the jack and handle and reattempted the prescriptive solution. Once: crash! Twice: crash! A third time: crash! But this time the car rolled forward a few inches. I threw the jack and handle in the trunk, leaped behind the wheel, and began a high-speed, white-knuckle run north on snow-clogged High Street while declining, politely, to sing harmony to "Heart of My Heart."

Peeling into the parking area in front of Bradley Hall, one of Ohio State's two '50s-era Virgin Vaults, I steered Ladylove up to the front door and waited in terrible silence for Mrs. Brown, the dorm mother, to arrive, seething, at the blacked-out entrance and open the door. I let Mrs. Brown deliver just enough of her "you're-going-straight-to-hell" speech to take some of the heat off Ladylove and raced back to the car.

Driving the cursed Icemobile back to the Phi Delt house, I climbed up to my room, threatened bodily harm to an assortment of brothers who, in my absence, were using my room as a saloon and who protested their expulsion with lurid threats, fed my monkey (we'll talk about him later, too) and fell, exhausted, into bed.

Some kinda night. And all for a buck.

¹ A later effort branding initiative would add "The" to the university's name.

ON AIR

NEED TO LOOK OLDER? Pose with a pipe. Ken tried unsuccessfully, for years, to smoke a pipe, but could never keep one lit.

The year, I'm guessing, was 1949 or '50. That would make me ten or eleven years old. Once again the season was winter, or at least the start of one—the opening act of another gray and windswept five months in the lives of my considerable family of brother, parents, aunts, uncles, and cousins in Toledo. Hanging onto the western end of Lake Erie by its fingertips, Toledo is just able to withstand the Alberta Clippers that come raging out of Canada each winter to skim the wind-driven froth from the lake and dump it as snow on Cleveland, Buffalo, and points east.

My mother and I were setting out that afternoon on what was by then a familiar Friday routine. Dad had driven our only car to the office that morning as he did each workday. To meet him for an end-of-week celebration, Mom and I would board the Old Orchard bus for a trip downtown and dinner at Grace Smith's Cafeteria, after which we'd all return home in the family car.

The whole operation had a military precision about it that I know gladdened my father's Teutonic heart. Born and raised in Toledo, he was one of eight children of an immigrant German father. His mother, born in Chicago, was herself first generation American, also born of German immigrants.

Adding to Dad's enjoyment of our weekly troop movement was the fact that he served as a 2nd Lieutenant in World War I.

Once, when it was necessary for us to locate the car downtown without him, he left a series of chalk arrows on the sidewalks leading from the cafeteria to our car parked at a curb several blocks away. But this day, for all its planning, the rendezvous failed. As we walked into Smith's Cafeteria, Dad was nowhere in sight.

My mother assumed, correctly as it turned out, that Dad

had simply been delayed leaving the office, something that seldom occurred in the life of the Director of Health and Physical Education for Toledo Public Schools. But what to do with her restive young son, who was eager to be in the cafeteria line savoring the newly-won privilege of filling his own plate? Ever inventive, with a conviction that rules, while good did not always apply to her, Mom determined to fill the time until Dad's arrival by leading me out of the cafeteria, up the block, through the street door, and up the dimly lit stairs of the business immediately adjacent. Though I never thought to ask her in later life, I'm confident she had never been there before nor even knew what the business was or did. The locus of our impromptu visit turned out to be the broadcast studios of WTOL Radio.

Now, more than a few winters have passed since the one of which I write, but I remember the scene that greeted us at the top of the stairs as if I had seen it this morning. We were in a lobby— small, unoccupied, and unlighted, owing to the lateness of the day. In the middle of the lobby was a round, high-backed sofa, its cushions facing outward, so that someone sitting on it was able to view what was happening in the surrounding studios.

Directly beyond the sofa, behind a large glass window, a man holding a sheaf of papers sat at a table, reading aloud.

In front of him, a microphone hanging from a boom was capturing his words and bringing them, amplified, into the lobby where we stood. The realization that it was also bringing them to hundreds, perhaps thousands, of other listeners at that same instant thrilled me to the very center of my being.

The man at the microphone was part-narrating, part-acting an adventure that I knew well. It involved the perils of Santa Claus trying to free himself from one villain after another in order to be aloft with his sleigh-full of goodies on Christmas Eve. Presented nightly in serialized form (and annually without much change), it held the rapt attention of Toledo tots for many years and helped to speed the days before Christmas.

Coming suddenly face to face with broadcasting like this had a profound effect on me and surely set the course of the next twenty years of my life, though for the first ten of those years I could do little more than dream about someday being that man behind the microphone.

But every so often the dreaming took on more tangible dimensions.

When I was about twelve or thirteen, I was rummaging through a storeroom at my uncles' roofing company. Under a pile of cardboard I found a military surplus intercom system. Awash in green camouflage and remarkably heavy owing to its vacuum tube technology, it permitted the person seated at the base unit to send his voice over wires to one or more remote speakers that could, in turn, become microphones for returning voice messages. It wasn't precisely radio, but it took my imagination closer to broadcasting than it had ever been before.

I don't remember how I extorted the intercom from my uncles, but I did, and before long, I had built a makeshift studio in our garage. On a picnic table sat the base unit of the intercom, its power cord plugged into an electric socket dangling by a cord from the rafters overhead. Twin braided-copper wires ran away from the base unit, passing out the garage window and up to a speaker wedged into the crotch of a large elm tree in our backyard. With the volume turned up full, it was possible to hear a voice to a distance of perhaps twenty feet from the speaker, just short of what I'm sure would have constituted unacceptable infringement on the rights of my parents and our neighbors.

Next to the intercom on the picnic table was an RCA Victor 78-rpm tabletop phonograph that my older brother, Ted, had coaxed my parents into buying. With his collection of records, and I'm certain without his permission, I assembled the "stacks of wax" that mimicked the disc jockeys I heard and admired on WJR Detroit and CKLW Windsor. A windup alarm clock completed the studio appointments. When "the old hands on the clock" said it was time, I wedged a short piece of dowel onto the transmit/receive switch on the intercom to lock it into the transmit mode, spun my theme song (Woody Herman's "Leap Frog"), and welcomed all my listeners to *Ken's Den*, an hour of recorded music "for all you guys and gals out there."

Just what I said during those "broadcasts" has been lost to memory, but I'm pretty confident that my chatter was borrowed intact from things I heard on WJR's *Guest House* with Bud Guest or CKLW's *Make-Believe Ballroom* with Eddie Chase. For the commercials I read advertisements from our newspaper, *The Toledo Blade*. And for the next hour, I actually became one of my heroes—a real-life radio broadcaster. Happily, this was before the day when a well-meaning parent recording the whole thing on home video could, in later years, reduce these happy memories to the foolishness they undoubtedly were. I'm grateful to be able to remember these moments without the benefit of clarity.

High school passed without my coming into contact with radio, although a classmate of mine, Bill Blinn, landed a one-hour show on WTOL. Bill was a year ahead of me in school and

I remember listening to his show on Saturday mornings, usually while completing one of my father's interminable lists of chores for his second son. One Saturday I was assigned to wash the kitchen walls, a task I completed by pacing myself to Bill's broadcast—one wall every fifteen minutes. If I felt any envy for Bill at the time—and I'm sure I did—it was soon erased as Bill's remarkable gifts became evident.

Moving to Hollywood and working as William Blinn, Bill wrote for such memorable TV series as *Rawhide, Bonanza,* and *Gunsmoke;* created the TV series *Starsky and Hutch;* developed the series *Eight Is Enough;* won a Peabody Award for the 1971 TV adaptation of *Brian's Song* and a 1977 Emmy for the TV mini-series *Roots.* At this writing he remains active in his craft.

Fall of 1957 brought me to Ohio State, and a month or so later, to the door of WOIO Radio. Unlike Ohio State's professionally staffed Telecommunications Center, including WOSUAM/FM/TV, WOIO was a purely student enterprise. I presume that there was a faculty representative somewhere, but I have no idea who it might have been; I never met him.

Located in the basement of Derby Hall, WOIO was part classroom, part radio studios. Walking into the complex from the dimly lit hall, you first entered a conventional classroom with a desk at the front facing a number of chairs with attached writing surfaces. Difficult to squeeze into, impossible to write on if you were left-handed, these chairs were nevertheless standard issue in every high school and college classroom I ever entered. At WOIO they were also never occupied, except by mounds of coats and books.

Leading away from the classroom to the right was a door that opened into a sound lock for two studios. A sound lock is simply a small closet with additional doors opening out from it. By closing one door before you open the next, you create a dead space for sound so that outside noise doesn't follow you when entering a studio that might have a "live" microphone.

Passing through a door in the right side of the sound lock you entered a room that bore a passing resemblance to a network studio capable of producing radio drama. In addition to a pair of microphones hanging from booms, there was a sound table consisting of four 78-rpm turntables with five separately controlled pickup arms.

Each arm was capable of reaching one of the turntables and three of them could be used on either of two tables. The practical effect of this arrangement was that a recording of night sounds (crickets, wind, etc.) that might only last two minutes could be made to play indefinitely by simply cross-fading from one pickup arm near the end of the recording to a second arm that had been placed at the beginning of the same recording. Other effects (a coyote howling, a dog baying) could be introduced as needed from recordings cued and ready on the other tables.

Making use of the sound table and a recorded effects library, a skilled operator could create the combination of sounds needed to evoke even the most complex scene in a listener's mind. Orson Welles' sound technician convinced thousands of Americans that they were hearing Martian spacecraft in his infamous "War of the Worlds" broadcast. All that was required of the listener was to close her eyes and open her imagination.

The only problem with this wonderful studio was that it was an anachronism.

By the latter half of the 1950s, nighttime radio drama was dead and daytime drama ("soaps") were dying. I remember taking a course in broadcast law about this time that bore little resemblance to what was happening in the industry at that very moment.

A closer approximation of radio in a mid-sized market at the middle of the last century was located across the sound lock from the network studio. Turning left out of the lock you entered a tiny "combo" studio. Here there was neither room nor need for actors, directors, announcers, engineers, and sound effects technicians. Here, one person, and one person only, was the whole show. Combining all the responsibilities for studio operation, this one person was announcer, news and sports director, music librarian, host, and engineer. In later employment, I added to the tasks above the roles of telephone receptionist and transmitter engineer's assistant (I've made up the latter title even as my management made up the task, which required the logging of electrical valuations I never understood every thirty minutes to fulfill the station's licensing requirements.)

There was a third door leading out of the sound lock, this one to WOIO's tiny music library. And perched like a small safe on the floor of this room was the station's transmitter. WOIO did not broadcast its signal in the conventional sense, but rather piggybacked it onto the electrical current produced by Ohio State's very own generating plant. This meant that in order to hear the station, you had to a) own a radio that was powered by electrical current, not batteries—not too much of a reach in those pre-transistor days, and b) have the radio plugged into a socket that made use of OSU-generated electricity. Most of the dormitories did, though probably none of the fraternity and sorority houses.

The signal was supposed to be heard below standard broadcast frequencies at, say, 510 kilocycles. Owing to the fact that the transmitter was seldom serviced, it merrily threw out its signal at all of its harmonics as well: 1020, 1530, and a few others in between, making the station roundly hated by most dorm residents who frequently could hear no other station on their radios.

WOIO signed on each weekday afternoon at 4 p.m. and off each evening at 10. It was in the late evenings, following sign-off, that many of us made our audition tapes that we hoped would win us a job with the commercial stations downtown. WOIO program content included some news, some sports (emphasis Big Ten), and lots of record shows. Students who were interested could become broadcasters by simply presenting themselves to the student station manager and receiving a shift assignment, say Wednesdays between 5 and 6 p.m. The station manager to whom I presented myself was a splendid upperclassman who wore a permanently bemused look tinged with melancholy, as if someone had just stolen a girlfriend he didn't much care for.

Dick Murgatroyd was quiet, capable, and made for a career in broadcasting. Among his many post graduate positions were stints as producer, director, or talent with AVCO Broadcasting, Bob Hope Enterprises, Taft Broadcasting, Multimedia Broadcasting, and the ABC, CBS, and NBC television networks. For many years he was famously the producer of the Ruth Lyons and Bob Braun TV shows, which originated in the Cincinnati studios of WLW-T and were networked to WLW stations in other cities. He is, as I write this, the Kenton County (Kentucky) Judge/Executive.

Dick's most endearing quality was his absolute unflappability. Wandering into the WOIO studios after 4 p.m., he might spend a moment exchanging pleasantries with the staffer on duty, who was busily filling the afternoon with music. As Dick turned to leave the tiny combo, studio he might remark, "You *do* know you aren't on the air, don't you?" thereby reminding the staffer that he had forgotten to turn on the transmitter at the start of his shift.

My most memorable brush with Dick's equanimity came a few seasons after our year together at WOIO. I was then employed by WOSU Radio, where my tasks included doing the colorcasts of Ohio State football games for the Ohio State Football Network. Dick was a producer/director at WOSU-TV, and was preparing to telecast the Ohio State men's home basketball season. I was asked to provide color commentary, Darrell Wible would do the play-by-play, and Dick would direct the telecasts from WOSU-TV's antique remote bus parked outside and adjacent to the school's St. John Arena.

During one game, my attention was drawn to the fact that we were covering the action with only one camera.

At best we had only two cameras at our disposal: one, a follow camera to provide close-ups and a second camera that at any given time showed the active half of the floor. The director's task was to call for cuts back and forth between the two cameras to provide the viewer with seamless action without revealing the follow camera's sometimes frantic search for who-the-hell had the ball.

Assuming, I suppose, that my news would come as a surprise, I picked up the telephone that connected Darrell and me, seated at a small table close to the rafters inside the arena, with the remote bus parked outside and below us. Dick answered the phone. Mildly mocking what I remembered him saying to others, I said "You *do* know you've only got one active camera, don't you?" Dick let out a melancholy sigh and replied, "I do, and we hope to do something about it, just as soon as someone puts out the fire."

A goodly portion of the inside of the bus was in flames.

There was another reason why WOIO was not held in high regard by the dorm rats at Ohio State, and this had to do with the music played by the station. It may come as a surprise to younger readers to learn that, at a point within even the writer's lifetime, the favorite music of children and their parents was one and the same. Composers, lyricists, performing artists, and orchestras were mutually enjoyed by two, and sometimes three, generations in the same family. And the all-time arbiter of what constituted our favorite music was the weekly radio broadcast of *Your Hit Parade*.

The program made its debut over NBC in 1935, and each week artists such as Buddy Clark, Frank Sinatra, Eileen Wilson, Doris Day, and Dinah Shore presented live performances of the top songs in America "as determined by *Your Hit Parade* survey, which checks the best-sellers in sheet music and phonograph records, the songs most heard on the air and most played in the automatic coin machines—an accurate, authentic tabulation of America's taste in popular music."

In 1950, *Your Hit Parade* moved from radio to television, still sponsored by the American Tobacco Company's Lucky Strike cigarettes. But change was occurring that would bring about the end of *Your Hit Parade* in 1959, and underscore the dorm rats' displeasure with WOIO.

Some credit Elvis Presley and some The Beatles, but whatever the fountainhead, young people had found a sound of their own, and they were no longer content to sit by their parents' side and wait to learn which song "the survey found in first place." They already knew, and to give the matter added attraction, their parents hadn't a clue. Rock 'n roll was not only here to stay, it was also delivering a final and fatal blow to the multi-generational music of *Your Hit Parade.*

At the time of which I write, the music of the young was recorded almost exclusively on 45-rpm records and the music of their parents on LP albums. WOIO's music library was filled with nothing but albums.

Because it was the music we played, it also defined the artists whose careers we followed.

And so, on learning that Mantovani and his Orchestra would be coming to Columbus for a concert, and that he would be appearing the night before in Youngstown, Ohio, it seemed entirely appropriate to think in terms of a road trip to interview the great man. Properly done, the interview would air on WOIO the day of the concert, thereby scooping the other local media who would have to wait for his arrival before they could hope to talk with him.

For most of the middle years of the last century, the radio interview of popular recording stars was one of the supremely successful symbiotic relationships. The promoter of a concert or dinner club booking such an artist was eager for the publicity to encourage patronage of the event, the cost for which was usually nothing more than a pair of comp tickets or dinner for the interviewer. The recording artist, too, wanted "good numbers" to assure repeat bookings and to fatten his or her agent's bargaining power with other promoters. Then, too, an interview afforded the artist the opportunity to "plug" the newest recording, thereby adding to the couple of cents the sale of each record would put in his or her pocket. Finally, the radio interviewer desperately wanted the cachet that went along with interviewing a big name talent to demonstrate his or her ability to play in the big leagues to station management and listeners alike.

Armed with just such knowledge I brought up the subject with a couple of fraternity brothers at dinner. "Hey, how'd you like to drive with me to Youngstown tonight so I can interview Mantovani for the radio station?" Jack Eby and Dave Underwood were active members of the fraternity, whereas I was still a pledge.

Normally, this sort of temerity on the part of a pledge would earn him a night of shining the actives' shoes. But Jack and Dave were transfers from Case Western University in Cleveland, and for reasons I never understood, were regarded by their active brothers as something less because of it. More than a pledge, to be sure, but less than an indigenous chapter active. To me, Jack and Dave were just very accessible upperclassmen, and I formed a close friendship with them; Jack would one day be part of my wedding party.

Because he had an advanced calculus midterm the next morning, Jack wavered on hearing the invitation, but his few feeble protests were quickly brushed aside. We would be back in plenty of time for him to take the test, and he could have the whole back seat of the car for the trip. Bring along a flashlight and his calculus textbook and it would be as good as studying in his room. Within a matter of minutes we were off to WOIO to pick up a tape recorder and then onto the highways for the 170-mile trip to Youngstown.

As Dave navigated the darkened, pre-Interstate roads, I began to address a couple of considerations for the first time. Given the distance to be driven and the lateness of the hour, we would arrive too late to get our interview before the concert, and maybe even to hear the concert itself. The best we could hope for was to speak with the great man afterwards, perhaps at his hotel. Which raised the second consideration: I had no idea where he was staying.

We followed our headlights through the night, arriving in Youngstown shortly before 11, and immediately set about finding the biggest and best hotel in the city, reasoning that this is where the great man would choose to stay.

Exactly how we did this and when we finally located him, I don't recall, but find him we did. Or rather his entourage. He was dining, we were told, and would not be available for an interview. But such was the strength of the relationship between promoters, artists, and the media that we were offered an alternative interview—an opportunity to converse with Charles Stanley "Stan" Newsome. It was almost as good as talking with the great man himself.

Annunzio Paulo Mantovani was born in Venice, Italy, in 1905. The family was in England, where his father was playing with a touring opera company, when World War I broke out. Unable to return home, the family settled in, and at age fourteen the young Mantovani began studying the violin. Improbably, just two years later he was leading his own quintet. Shortly after, the group became a fixture at the Hotel Metropole, London, where it began to broadcast regularly. He became a Decca recording artist in 1940, and in 1951 formed the New Orchestra of forty musicians that would make his name famous in both England and the United States.

Often associated with the phrase "cascading strings," the Mantovani sound was slow, string-filled, and syrupy. It was also very popular. And, at that moment, it was being heard on the radio at almost every turning, thanks to its recording of Victor Young's theme from the Mike Todd movie spectacular, *Around the World in 80 Days.*

Against a barn-full of violins, the main theme was sung by a high, inordinately clear solo trumpet. Stan Newsome played that trumpet.

A short, wiry, and white-haired pixie of a man, Stan Newsome loved the idea of participating in our interview.

Or rather, he loved the camaraderie it instantly provided— three new companions to share drinks with before and after we talked. To steady his nerves, Stan drank one during the interview as well.

I asked the usual questions and Stan must have provided the usual answers—I don't remember anything particularly revealing coming from our discussion—and the interview was at an end. As we were packing to leave, the interviewee began interviewing us: Where and how did we live at Ohio State? My companions provided all the relevant information. We said our goodbyes and then it was back to Columbus, arriving about 4 a.m. I fell into bed for a few brief hours of sleep, then grabbed the tape of the interview and set off for the station. As quickly as I could, I cut the interview into logical segments, separating them with selections from Mantovani albums and concluding with "the" recording of *Around the World in 80 Days.* By the time the station signed on that afternoon, the interview was ready to air. I pitched the tape to the announcer on duty who agreed to air it, stuck around long enough to hear it actually broadcast, and then headed back to the fraternity house.

Jack had missed his midterm. In later years he would write me, "I was so exhausted after being up all night that I was unable to take the exam and threw myself on the mercy of the instructor. He found the tale I related about how I had spent the previous night and the bad company that I had been keeping so bizarre and creative that he excused me from the exam and accepted my course average to date as the score for the exam."

This small academic setback didn't hurt Jack's career.

He went on to hold a wide range of positions with Ford Motor Company between 1964 and 1995, retiring as Executive Director of Corporate Strategy. He was responsible for recommending and coordinating Ford's global strategies and overseeing mergers and acquisitions. Previously he had served as president of Ford Japan. As I write this, Jack is president of John T. Eby & Associates, a management consultancy in Bloomfield Hills, Michigan, that includes Sony as a client.

But the story is not over. Whatever my social or academic responsibilities for the balance of the day, I was not able to crawl back under the covers as I desperately desired. Now, late at night, as I wearily climbed the stairs to my room in the fraternity, I became aware of a riotous party going on somewhere in the house. Not for me; not tonight. But on reaching my door, I discovered the party was in my room. Half a dozen brothers and twice as many bottles of amber liquid were squeezed into the tiny space I shared with my monkey (really, I will discuss him later in this memoir). They all had their backs to me as I tried to wedge my way into the room.

The focus of the brothers' attention was none other than Stan Newsome, himself, who was holding court while seated on the edge of my bed. He had used the information provided to him the night before to find his way to the Phi Delt house following the concert. I smiled weakly, greeted everyone by name, and accepted a glass of something-and-ice. Within minutes the white noise of conversation, the warmth of the drink, and the endless hours without sleep began to take their toll and I could no longer keep my eyes open. Carefully, I moved to the foot of the bed, easing my body between the wall and Stan's back. In a matter of seconds, I was fast asleep.

I have no idea how long I was out when I was rudely shaken back to consciousness. As my eyes focused, I saw Stan hovering over me, his face a mask of scorn. With elaborate precision, so as not to spoil the moment by slurring his words, he pronounced the ultimate condemnation:

"Keller, you're a helluva host."

rehearsal

Chapter three

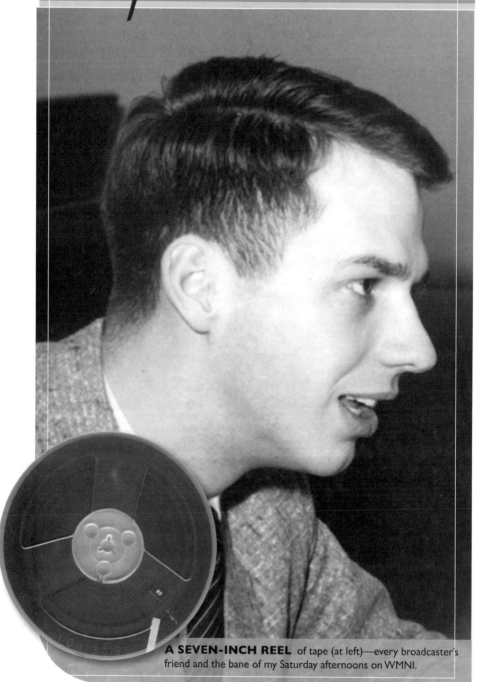

A SEVEN-INCH REEL of tape (at left)—every broadcaster's friend and the bane of my Saturday afternoons on WMNI.

I don't remember his name, and I don't suppose he remembers her name, but the two of them were caught in cupid's embrace on the boss's sofa, and that's how I got the job at WMNI. That was the thing about radio in the middle of the last century; you were either doing three things at once or nothing at all, and either could get you into trouble, as this chapter will explain.

The subject of the above paragraph, like I, was a student at Ohio State working part-time in broadcasting. He had already made the leap from student radio to commercial radio; I was waiting in the wings. Lured, I imagine, by the promise of large blocks of free time during a weekend shift, he had brought a lady friend to the studio to keep him company. He had not counted on a surprise visit from the boss.

Such diversions were not uncommon among announcers. I'm told that NBC network announcers in New York played a form of "chicken" during the twenty-nine minutes between their golden-throated orations. Forsaking the announcers' lounge they would ride the elevators up and down Rockefeller Center, hoping to arrive back in the announce booth with exactly no time to spare before the on-air light flashed on.

The boss in our story was William R. Mnich, erstwhile car salesman who had diversified his investments by starting a new radio station. That last sentence deserves a closer look. When I arrived in Columbus, conventional wisdom held that the city had all the AM radio stations its crowded dial could accommodate.

To his credit, Bill somehow managed to get the Federal Communications Commission to agree to license a new station at 920 kilocycles (later kilohertz). The "W" in WMNI denotes a radio station located east of the Mississippi; the remaining three letters are the first three letters of Bill's last name (pronounced mih-NICK).

With license in hand, Bill set about building a studio and staffing his station. In both cases, no expense was too small. Because he had had to mortgage his house, as well as borrow a great deal of money to launch his fledgling radio enterprise, Bill's new station had to make do with cast-offs and hand-me-downs. Take the tape machines, for example. In those pre-digital days, professional quality tape recorders, referred to as decks, were a vital part of any station's list of studio equipment. They were used both to record and playback program content and commercials. Because they frequently needed to be activated by the announcer from his seated position before the microphone, the best decks had remote start/stop/record buttons, as well as silent start-up.

WMNI's, by contrast, were a mismatched pair of used machines never intended for studio use. Neither could be started or stopped except by getting up from the microphone and planting yourself firmly in front of them. One, a Crown, was built for home use and required a massive amount of force to engage its drive mechanism. The other, a Magnecorder, was built for editing and featured an exposed playback head. It had the distressing habit of coasting after you stopped it, making an announcer sound foolish if he lead to a tape, only to have the playback start several seconds into the first sentence. A practical demonstration of these shortcomings will follow. I mentioned earlier that in broadcasting you were either too busy or not busy enough. Let's take a moment to consider the former.

On arriving at the station for a typical shift, job one for the announcer was to select the music to be played that day. To do this, you entered the music library and began assembling a mix of 45-rpm records and LP albums, literally building "a stack of wax" (actually vinyl) according to the station's music policy. Such a policy might dictate that a male vocalist was always to be followed by an instrumental selection that in turn would be followed by a female vocalist, a Broadway cast or Hollywood soundtrack selection, a group vocal, and finally a novelty number, and that this sequence was to be followed in endless rotation. Program directors made their livings, and reputations, by developing just such arcane formulae. But even as I entered broadcasting in the late 1950s, some stations were abandoning a full music policy for a top-40 formula that literally reduced the size of the music library to a wire rack holding no more than forty 45-rpm records.

Once you had "pulled" your show it was time to check the news hooks. Day and night, teletype machines delivered an endless highway of yellow paper filled with news, sports, and feature items from United Press International and Associated Press into newsrooms across the country. News directors separated the stories by tearing the endless feed of paper against the edge of a concrete mason's trowel or metal ruler, then spiking the stories on hooks according to their content: national, international, state, city, sports, weather, features. Feature material ranged from updates on the lives of celebrities to simple human interest stories. Announcers who were about to be faced with hours of airtime to fill wanted all the feature stories they could find.

Finally, armed with as many recordings as you could carry, you entered the studio to become the "sound" of your station, usually for a period of four to five hours. Weekend shifts could last much longer; I once worked sixteen hours straight.

Recordings of the day lasted about two and a half minutes per track. Here's what you did during each of those 150 seconds. To begin, if you had just read or played a commercial or public service announcement, you had to enter that fact in the station's broadcast log. You did so using up to twelve digits, indicating the hour, minute, and second it began and the hour, minute, and second it ended (3:15:20-3:16:20). If you happened to run two commercials back-to-back, you were looking at as many as twenty-four digits. Next, you selected the piece of music to follow the one that was now playing, placed it on the turntable and, using the cue circuit, rotated the turntable to find the start of the recording, then back-cued it half a turn so that it wouldn't "wow" on start-up. Then you checked the log to see what was to happen during the next break. A recorded commercial? Locate and cue the proper disc, tape, or tape cartridge. A live commercial? Look it over and rehearse any tough words or phrases. A weather forecast? Phone the weather bureau for the current temperature and humidity. News headlines? Leave the studio and race to the teletypes, grab the most recent stories to read but also spike the earlier stories for various feature broadcasts, such as farm prices and stock reports. Without time to read, much less rehearse, the headlines before reading them on-air (a practice referred to as "rip 'n read"), you prayed there were no typos; no unfinished or ungrammatical sentences; no six-syllable or foreign words; no Russian names that were suddenly in the news that would betray the fact that you and your audience were coming across this information for the very first time—together.

By now the recording that's been playing is into its final seconds. But the telephone is flashing and you're expected to answer it (it could be the station manager calling in to complain about something you said or did. If not, it's probably a listener on the same mission). The transmitter readings are already late, meaning you'll have to fake them yet again. Up ahead three or four minutes is a tape program you have to locate and cue or else leave "dead air" while you scramble to do it then. And you still haven't found the time to pee, which first became an issue almost an hour ago.

In radio, in the middle of the last century, in middle America, when you were busy, you were very, very busy. Management believed that downsizing (a word not yet coined) was its only defense against the flight of commercial dollars that were quickly abandoning radio for the new, exciting—and for the moment inexpensive—medium of TV. This elevated a willingness to work long hours for little money to the very pinnacle of a radio announcer's employment credentials. It also set to burning the fires of my personal hell—Saturdays on WMNI.

The mornings would begin calmly enough with several hours of a record show and the occasional break for news and sports. But about 9:30, a strange assortment of people carrying a variety of large suitcases would start filtering into the hall outside the on-air studio. I would know they were there when some would actually come into the studio, greeting me with questions or a request to leave their suitcases—actually instrument cases—in some unoccupied corner, the hallway already being clogged with the same. The fact that I might have the microphone open seldom deterred them from extending to me the heartiest, and earthiest, of greetings.

These were the students of Whitey Lunzar, music shop proprietor, teacher, and by reason of payment to Mr. Mnich, owner of two hours of Saturday morning airtime on WMNI. In keeping with Mr. Mnich's frugality, there was a miniscule production studio adjacent to the on-air studio, its plywood walls only partly covered with sound-absorbing acoustic tiles. As the hour approached 10, I watched through a small plate glass window as the production studio filled with an assortment of guitars, mandolins, fiddles, and accordions, each in the grasp of its earnest and sometimes terrified owner.

Once on the air, Whitey became the host of his program, introducing his charges with glowing praise for their musicianship and extravagant claims about their futures in show business. My on-air studio now became a control room, and my task was to "ride gain" on the fledgling stars. Riding gain meant controlling the volume levels for both voice and instruments—no easy task when a single microphone had to suffice for both. Sending too "hot" a signal to the transmitter could trigger a limiter that would quickly (and ruthlessly) drop the broadcast volume, making the performer appear to disappear from the radio for several seconds until the limiter decided it was safe to restore full volume. Sending too low a signal to the transmitter would effectively produce the same result.

Once a performer's volume was set, I chanced running out to the teletype to grab a handful of news and sports for the next report, praying that this particular rendition of "Red River Valley" didn't contain a whoop or a yodel that would send the transmitter into overload. Back in the control room I'd actually have a chance to read the news to myself before reading it on the air.

And so, with many assorted clunks and bonks as accordions, banjos, and various body parts collided with the microphone stand (less expensive than a boom that would have kept the mic out of harm's way), Whitey Lunzar's two hours of showcasing his students and plugging his wares came to a close. For me, the day was just shifting into high gear.

Now, an exquisite ballet was about to begin during which I would conduct an afternoon record show (note description earlier this chapter) while, at the same time, recording the Notre Dame football game of the day from the ABC Radio Network for delayed broadcast. At a fully staffed station, I would have conducted the record show while a studio engineer recorded the football game. At a fully equipped station, I would have conducted the record show while the football game, in its entirety, was recording on a single ten-inch tape at 3.75 inches per second. But the careful reader will recall that WMNI did not own a studio-quality tape deck capable of recording a ten-inch tape. What I had at my disposal were two bloody mismatched machines that could record only on seven-inch reels at 7.5 inches per second. As a consequence, every half-hour or so, regardless of whatever else may have been happening at the moment, I had to leap up from the microphone, run to the tape decks and switch one machine off while I switched the other on, hoping I did so during a brief pause in the play-by-play. Then back to the records, the log, the commercials, the news headlines and weather, and the telephone.

And so the afternoon passed in a flurry of activity while I sought to reassure the listeners with my voice that, hey, everything's cool and isn't it great to be laid back and listening to these tunes together?

Eventually it became 4 p.m.—time to end the record show and begin the rebroadcast of the Notre Dame game. With luck, the game was over, and both tape decks were available for playback. In those pre-TV days, before commercials made a game run all afternoon, this was at least possible. But sometimes the game was still in progress, meaning I had to use one tape deck for playback while still recording on the other—a sticky proposition when it was time to segue between the decks to achieve a seamless broadcast. If the first playback tape ended and the second machine was still recording, it was necessary to cut the volume on the first machine at the console in front of the announcer's microphone, race to the first machine, rip the tape from its spindles, put the second tape on the same spindles and thread the tape over the playback head, roll the tape, and race back to the console to bring the volume up on the new tape. At best this was a fifteen-second enterprise, rather a long period of dead air between "He's at the thirty, the twenty, the ten" and "Touchdown!"

For good measure, I was responsible for inserting local commercials over the network commercials during the rebroadcast. To do this, I needed to be alert to the play-by-play announcer's sometimes hurried decision to cue a commercial break: "We'll be back to Norte Dame football after this message," or words to that effect. In the 1950s, the pace of a football game was still determined by the opposing coaches, not by a TV producer, and broadcasters had to find commercial breaks where they could. Was there an injury? An equipment problem? A dog on the field? Cue the break and hope nothing of consequence to the game happened in the next sixty seconds.

Once a break cue was given, I had to cut the audio from the tape deck while I read a local commercial in its place. To make sure I rejoined the network broadcast cleanly—that is, in the moment of silence between the end of the network commercial and the resumption of play-by-play—I listened to the audio from the tape deck (the network feed) in one of my two earphones while I listened to myself reading the commercial in the other. I became fairly adept at concentrating on what I was saying while still reserving a small portion of my consciousness for what I was hearing. It was an exercise that went a long way toward preparing me to be a husband and father of two.

The nightmare scenario in all of this is as follows: The game has run long; you are still recording on one machine as you playback on the other; you've started reading a commercial when, in your earphones, the network feed disappears because the playback tape has run out. Now you must a) complete the reading of the commercial, b) cut your mic, leap up, and race to the tape deck carrying your earphones with you, c) rip off the used tape and replace it with the next playback tape, carefully threading the tape over the playback head, d) start the tape as you jam your earphones into the machine to listen to the playback, e) fast-forward through the remainder of the network commercial to the start of the play-by-play, f) race back to the console and bring the audio back up. With luck, you've pulled the whole thing off with only thirty seconds of dead air, an eternity in radio terms.

The odds against all this happening at the same time were very great. It's a wonder to me, therefore, that it happened as often as it did.

Eventually, the game came to its end and with it my Saturday shift. I would leave the station feeling as if I had run a marathon. But if Saturdays were non-stop, balls-to-the-wall activity, Sundays were the exact opposite, bringing with them another cause of exhaustion: boredom.

By contrast with Saturday's crowded hall, Sunday's was quiet and unoccupied. I used the space as a walking track to try to relieve the tedium; there was little else to do. Following sign-on, Sunday's log was filled with half-hour paid religious programs requiring only that I make a station break every thirty minutes. Because they were recorded, I wasn't even responsible for keeping the volume constant. Sometime during the morning we went live to a local church for an hour's coverage of its services, but all that meant was that I didn't need to make the station break on the half-hour. The morning crept by with exquisite slowness.

At noon I was free, but not for the day; I was scheduled to work the last three hours of Sundays as well. Early on a wonderful and breathtaking idea began to form in my hormone-ravaged mind. WMNI's studios, as I mentioned, were on the top floor of the Southern Hotel. Beneath them were floor upon floor of rooms for rent, most of them unoccupied. Since I needed to be back in harness a mere eight hours later, why even leave the hotel? Why not rent a room and invite Ladylove to come and use the time to study with me? Biology, I hoped, would be our subject of choice.

And so it came to be. As I entered the hotel on Sunday mornings I would request a room for the day from the clerk in the lobby.

Faced with inventing a name for the register, I settled on one that had just a touch of familiarity so as not to seem as if I were hiding anything. No John Smith for me. Adding a bogus middle initial to the name of Princess Margaret's former lover produced a name that had the added advantage of employing the initials of my fraternity, which went along nicely with its address, which I also used on the registration form. And so Peter D. Townsend became a frequent Sunday guest of the Southern Hotel.

Ever hopeful that an afternoon of "studying" might actually include some studying, Ladylove would meet me with an armload of books when I picked her up at her dormitory. And maybe that first time alone, together, in a hotel room, we actually opened a book or two. But in a tiny room dominated by a bed and containing little else, we were drawn to it with all the passion of youth. And there, surrounded by the biggest and ugliest flowers ever inflicted on harmless wallpaper, I discovered the most beautiful architecture of all of God's creation: the rises and falls, the flat places and curved, the light places and dark of a woman's body.

More than forty years later, while doing genealogical research, I discovered that the consortium of immigrant German businessmen who built The Great Southern Fireproof Hotel and Opera House was headed by my great uncle, Nicholas Schlee.

I lost my virginity in Uncle Nick's hotel.

To the extent that Ladylove got any studying done, it was during the three hours that I worked before Sunday signoff when she was left alone in the room.

Those may have been the longest hours of any shift, knowing that she was only partly dressed and just a few floors below me. One cold and lonely night I reached for the tape that was to fill the last thirty minutes of the broadcast day, only to discover that it was nowhere to be found. Remembering that curfew that night for Ladylove was still ninety minutes away, and being very much in need of additional studying, I called the engineer at the transmitter and suggested that, absent a program for the final thirty minutes of the day, we might just as well pull the plug and go home. He readily agreed, I read the station sign-off, played the National Anthem, and took the elevator down to my Ladylove's waiting arms.

The next day I was summoned to Mr. Mnich's office where I was, appropriately, read the riot act. What had I been thinking?

Even given the missing program I should have filled with music to the end of the broadcast day. Didn't I know that signing off early might attract the attention of the FCC and put the station's license in jeopardy? I fully expected such a chat and decided in advance that whatever the consequences it was worth it, though I confess I hadn't thought of the possible consequences to the station. I may have grown a bit that day.

As the holidays approached at the end of 1958, a series of events conspired to create a week that will live a lifetime in my memory. Our afternoon man, Bob Linville, had somehow attracted the attentions of a woman who was living in the hotel while some fire damage to the kitchen of her home was being repaired. Because she would be in the hotel for an extended stay, her insurance company had agreed to put her up in what passed for a suite at the Southern.

I don't remember her real name, but I do remember that she had aspirations of a career in radio and was prepared to call herself Jill Jarvis.

Both divorced, Bob and Jill became instantly attached at the hip and, I was soon to learn, at various other points of their anatomies as well. With many real and imagined staff illnesses, as well as planned vacations for the rest of the announcers, Bob and I became almost the entire air staff of the station from Christmas to New Year's Eve. When one of us wasn't on the air, the other was. Between shifts, Jill's suite was our clubhouse.

As I think of that incredible week, it isn't just the countless boxes of pizza from Papajacs that I remember, or the still life of multi-colored beer and bourbon bottles, some upright, some on their sides, that littered every surface of the suite. It isn't the constant pulsing of high-energy activity followed by physical and mental exhaustion, only to be followed by the need to once more find the energy to perform. It isn't even the heady presence of Ladylove meeting me and loving me at all hours of the day and night, something heretofore denied us. I remember most the dawning of the wonderful and exhilarating and terrifying realization that my youth had finally and irretrievably ended, and, ready or not, my adult life had begun.

Chapter four

MEET THE FULL-TIME AIR STAFF of WMNI circa 1958 as they hosted a local sock hop. Sporting matching black bow ties, from left, afternoon host Bob Linville, program director Harv Morgan, and morning man Mike Gavin.

Bob Linville is the reason I flunked out of Ohio State.

OK, maybe not the whole reason—I had set the table with several quarters of marginal grades. Bob simply pulled the tablecloth out from under the plates and glasses and sent them crashing to the floor. And the truth of the matter is that I didn't so much flunk out as one quarter I simply failed to show up for too many classes. It was a distinction the university failed to recognize and at the end of spring quarter 1959 I was sent a Notice of Academic Disenrollment (I thought the last word odd at the time and am amused that even my spell check fails to recognize it).

The first half of my weekday split-shift at WMNI involved "riding the board"—doing whatever was required in the way of programming—between noon and 1 p.m. I've forgotten just what this entailed, but my guess is it involved providing listeners with a mixture of news, sports, stock updates, and weather from many different sources. At any rate, seconds before 1 p.m. I was to give a station break and a time check and then spin Bob's theme song, at which point Bob was to walk through the studio door to begin his afternoon shift. I would then leave the station and drive furiously up High Street to begin afternoon classes at Ohio State.

The problem was that, quite often, his theme song ended without Bob walking through the door. Recognizing his propensity for late arrivals Bob had chosen a very long theme, something on the order of five to six minutes in length.

During that time I watched the door the way a condemned man watches the phone next to the warden. Sometimes Bob would sweep in at the last second, plump down behind the mic and, with a cherubic smile at me, announce that "Once again, for all you folks who requested it, that was the complete recording of 'Sing, Sing, Sing.'" Other times he simply didn't show up at all. I could, of course, have insisted on leaving anyway. Once or twice doing that and Bob would have been gone, a new and presumably more responsible man would have taken his place, and I could have gone to my afternoon classes without incident. I must say the thought never occurred to me.

The first time Mr. Mnich with solemn eyes told me that he had no other on-air staff available and that I would have to carry the ball for the station, I was flattered and thrilled beyond thinking about academic consequences. I did the show, I did it reasonably well, and because I did, I set a precedent that soon became standard operating procedure; when Bob failed to show up I was the substitute host.

As I looked more and more toward a career in broadcasting, the afternoon shifts on WMNI became a wonderful internship. Under Mr. Mnich's tutelage, I learned that the ending "g" in gerunds were really meant to be sounded. No more walkin' and talkin' for me; I became a walking, talking guy. He also saw to it that I identified and abandoned the few northwest Ohioisms I brought with me to Columbus, such as saying crick for creek. But I knew that when news of Ohio State's decision reached my parents, without so much as a word being spoken, I would be on my own financially. And for this I needed a better paying job.

The jungle drums among broadcasters beat loud and late; there are probably few industries in which more hiring and firing takes place than radio and TV. So I soon learned that WTVN Radio was looking for a late night man.

As WMNI was Columbus' newest AM radio station, WTVN was, and still is, its oldest. Licensed to broadcast April 29, 1922, with the call letters WBAV, WTVN is tied with WBAX in Wilkes-Barre, Pennsylvania, as the sixtieth oldest surviving station in the United States.[2]

For me, there were several advantages to the WTVN position. I would be leaving behind the start-up studios of WMNI for one of the best appointed stations in Columbus, with broadcast quality studio equipment and a larger and more varied music library. I would also be saying adieu to frantic Saturday mornings with Mr. Lunzar's B-flat barbarians. I would be working as part of a team that included some old and respected names in Columbus broadcasting. And I would have a significantly larger potential audience; at 5,000 watts WTVN could be heard in almost all of Ohio's eighty-eight counties, especially at night when I would be on-air. Included among those counties would be Lucas, home of my old high school buddies and even a former Ladylove or two. I had made up the difference between Bill Blinn and myself, if you ignored the groundwork Bill was quietly laying in Hollywood.

Program Director Bob Adkins interviewed me and, upon offering me the position, mentioned the princely sum of $1.50 an hour. I was delighted. Two hours a night times five nights a week plus eight hours on the weekend meant more than just thirty-six dollars a week before taxes; it meant if I could talk brother Jim Snook into letting me keep my room in the fraternity house across the summer, living rent free in exchange for providing him company in his role as caretaker, I would have until fall to find a permanent job that would launch me full-time into the work force.

Night broadcasting on WTVN was a delight. The pace of everything was slower than during the day. Words could be chosen with greater care and a closer intimacy forged with listeners. This understanding did not occur to me as a conscious thought but rather as the consequence of reading the mail that began arriving at the station in my name.

Listeners were pleased by the selection of music I offered and wanted me to know what they were doing as they listened. I've kept a number of postcards and notes from my years of night broadcasting without being sure why I selected the ones I did while discarding the rest.

"It is seldom that I am moved to letter writing, especially to someone I have never met or may never have the pleasure of meeting," began one. "Your program this evening featuring Leroy Anderson was wonderful." From a young mother: "When I wrote you before I told about my son Stephen who was then just a baby. Your music put him to sleep each night. Now he has grown so much, and on March 13 we will celebrate his first birthday." "I think that the music you pick is perfect for the time of night," wrote another. "I normally listen while I study, and I find your programming both restful and appropriate."

The mail would sometimes bring disconcerting letters. The following, written in pencil on a form provided by the Ohio Penitentiary and dated September 27, 1960, was sent to me in care of WRFD, my first full-time employer. "Dear Sir, In regards to the progran of Sep 26, you done George Gershwin,s Porgy and Bess. But in doing so it was also educational with the dates and places. this request is frakly out of the way but I would appreciate it very much if you would be kind enough to send me a copy of that scrip the same as you did over the air. I listen to (you) every day because (you) play music of intrest and class. I thank you and will await you reply and scrip. Yours truly, Joe Louis Cosby."

Three days after writing his letter and before I could reply, Mr. Cosby was executed at the Ohio Penitentiary, walking, according to *The Columbus Dispatch*, "with apparent calm to the electric chair" for the slaying of a Cleveland shoe store manager during an armed robbery.

Sometimes the letters were simply sad. One that has remained with me, both in fact, and in memory, was written in a large and flowing hand on white tablet paper. Requesting that I play "music especially for tired farm women" she continued, "I guess maybe I am Different—a little girl with a brand New Dress—Expects God to Notice it—to love its soft folds as she does. To Notice the

The letter sent to Keller from Joseph Cosby, an inmate in the Ohio Department of Rehabilitation.

things she does—they are important aren't they—or is it more Important to take a Dress for Granted. I never had a comin-out dress—even my Wedding Dress Was shop Worn. So many things I've never had."

WTVN was not only a great place to work, it was also a great place to go to watch and learn.

Much has been made of former President Reagan's years in broadcasting during which, among other things, he "called" baseball games from a studio located miles from the ballpark using game statistics provided by a ticker. WTVN had its own master of bogus baseball broadcasting.

Joe Hill was tall and courtly with a self-effacing shyness and a wonderful, warm radio voice. He was, for years, the voice of Jets baseball.

Columbus was a founding franchise of the American Association in 1902. Its team, then called the Senators, later became the Red Birds and remained in the AA until the St. Louis Cardinals moved the franchise to Omaha at the end of the 1954 season.

Soon after, the Pittsburgh Pirates established a new farm team in Columbus, naming it the Jets and making it part of the International League. Today, owned by the Washington Nationals and called the Clippers, the team remains a competitive member of the IL.

Watching Joe call a broadcast was a study in how baseball is played and a reminder to me of why I have no patience for the game. Joe sat at a microphone with two turntables, one to his left and one to his right. The turntable on the right contained a recording of the next commercial to be aired. The one on the left

Death Row photo of Joe Louis Cosby. The Ohio Department of Rehabilitation and Correction maintains a website of photos of those they have executed. In several of the photos, men are wearing the same tie.

The Ohio Penitentiary. Pastel tints on this vintage post card soften the gray walls of the prison, scene of the worst prison fire in U.S. history. On April 21, 1930, 322 inmates perished. It was demolished in 1998 to make way for a sports arena complex.

played what was called an ET, or electrical transcription. It was simply a half-hour recording of baseball crowd noise. Played with low volume it was the happy hubbub of an expectant crowd. Bring the volume up suddenly and the same sound was a crowd on its feet watching to see if a fly ball left the park. As Joe ad-libbed a realistic account of the game from the meager statistics provided by the ticker, he alternately raised and lowered the volume control on the crowd noise. The effect to closed eyes was eerily like being at the park.

When he had used all the statistics from his last gleaning of the ticker, Joe would get up and shamble out of the studio, down the hall and into the office where the ticker was housed to retrieve another few feet of paper data.

On his way back to the studio you could count on him to spend a moment or two in pleasant conversation before returning to the microphone. All the while the ET kept up the illusion that you were at the park just waiting for the next big moment in the game. The fact that listeners accepted these prolonged lapses in play-by-play as part of the mystique of the game was simply incomprehensible to me, and to this day I cannot watch more than an inning or two of baseball before I need to be somewhere else.

The studio that Joe sat in was one of two or three that were clustered about a large and blacked-out control room—a holdover from the days of network radio, when all of the complex engineering functions of the station were carried out by studio engineers seated at the large horseshoe-shaped console. Floor-to-ceiling plate glass windows permitted the talent in the studios and the engineers in the control room to communicate via hand and eye signals. As noted earlier, the broadcasters of the '50s were their own engineers, simultaneously performing the functions of talent and engineer. Roaming about the old control room was a stroll through radio's storied past, and the fact that I could never find the switch to the overhead lights (what light did find its way into the room came from the lights in the surrounding combo studios) seemed to me an apt commentary on the then-present state-of-radio-art.

My task at WTVN was to fill the last hour of each day and the first hour of the next with music, and nobody thought it necessary to tell me how to do it. Absent strict music programming guides, I felt free to experiment when I could.

One of the spring rituals at Ohio State was Greek Week, during which, among other events, fraternities and sororities would compete in a song competition. Practiced and presented with all the intensity of an athletic meet, these "sings" were fun to participate in and often a delight to hear.

One day I ran into an old high school classmate named Brad Kinney who had just directed his fraternity's singers to first place in that year's competition. I asked him if he would be willing to bring the group to WTVN to sing a couple of songs on the air. He readily agreed, and the next night, at the arranged time, about 20 young men began pouring through the studio door. Worth noting is that WTVN's studios were on the someteenth floor of the Buckeye Federal Savings and Loan building in the middle of downtown Columbus. The fact that 20 college-age men could enter a darkened building in the middle of the night and ride elevators up to a live broadcast studio without anyone challenging them with regard to their plans or destination tells a good bit about life in middle America in the middle of the last century.

Between the songs being performed live that evening, I wanted
to ask Brad a few questions about preparing his singers, but Brad
had done too much celebrating following their victory and had
lost his voice. He guessed he could croak out a few short answers.
When I asked him how hard it had been to coach his fraternity to
victory, he thought for a moment, and then, without saying a word,
made an elaborate swipe with his hand across the area in front of
his genitals. The allusion to "sweat of his balls" was not lost on
anyone in the studio, but the resulting laughter must have puzzled
the listeners. I answered the question for him, making up some
lame approximation of "It had taken a lot of hard work."

The evening of live songs with male voices went so well that
the next day I extended the same opportunity to the winning
sorority. It, too, agreed, and a few nights later I was happily at the
center of twenty-some coeds crowded oh-so-snugly into my studio.

With my days free, courtesy of Ohio State's Department of
Academic Affairs, I began looking for something to fill them. In
later years I would have searched for a job to help pay the family
bills. But being single and able to live, if barely, on my WTVN
income, I would spend a small part of each day making the
audition rounds and the remainder hanging out at the fraternity
house. When this began to wear thin, I auditioned for a part in a
local theatre production of Lawrence and Lee's *Inherit the Wind*.

Jerome Lawrence was an Ohio State graduate, and Robert E.
Lee attended Ohio Wesleyan University, but neither knew the other
until they met during World War II and together founded Armed
Forces Radio. Following the war, they created radio programs for
CBS, including the series *Columbia Workshop*. Their first theatrical
collaboration was writing the book for *Look, Ma, I'm Dancin'!* and

their second, *Inherit the Wind*, was produced on Broadway in 1955. Later works included the book for the musical *Auntie Mame* and *The Night Thoreau Spent in Jail*, which premiered at Ohio State and was directed by Dr. Roy Bowen. In 1959, the same Dr. Bowen was directing *Inherit the Wind* for Columbus' Players Club (later Player's Theatre).

I had not yet learned that having a good speaking voice was not the same thing as being an actor, though the beginning of that awareness was only a matter of months away. Still armed with the misconception that one gift was as good as the other, I showed up for Dr. Bowen's auditions with high hopes.

It's unlikely that I would have been given a role in this excellent retelling of the famous Scopes Monkey Trial if it weren't for my one special talent; I owned a monkey.

In those unenlightened days before animal rights legislation, it was possible to order rare animals through the mail, and sometime during 1958 I had done just that, sending my check and fraternity address to a company that promised to send me a live Capuchin monkey in return. On the day of its arrival I was saddened to find it dead in its shipping crate. But true to the company's promise of live delivery, a second monkey was soon on its way. This one arrived healthy and feisty and more than ready to take on the challenges of life in a fraternity house.

Peanuts was a survivor and lived life on his own terms. His small, brown face always seemed to be asking, "You want a piece of me?" Home was a large brass cage on the desk in my room. The door was always open, and in any case, he had figured out how to open it within hours of his arrival. By day it was a place to eat, relieve himself (if that suited his immediate purpose), and enter voluntarily when he had had enough of his frequent visitors. At night he would sit atop the cage until I got undressed and into bed, then leap from the desk to the bed and burrow under the covers, eventually settling into the space at the small of my back. He quickly taught me the penalty for sleeping in any position other than on my side. One night I awoke to a searing pain in my middle back and in the morning discovered a perfect set of tiny teeth prints at the exact point of my discomfort.

Though Peanuts and I were roommates, we were never really friends.

He accepted my feeding him and sharing my bed in an unheated room as little more than his due, which, of course, it was. Quickly learning my routine, which on his arrival still included morning classes at Ohio State, he would watch in sullen silence as I donned my Midshipman's uniform for an eight o'clock Naval Science class. One morning, face to the mirror as I tied my tie, I felt a sting in the back of my neck. As I turned to search for the cause, I caught the second cufflink, thrown with perfect aim and anger, full in the forehead.

My role in *Inherit the Wind* was non-speaking. I was to wander onto the stage in an early crowd scene with Peanuts on my shoulder. Different members of the cast would address remarks to Peanuts or to me, but neither of us were required to answer. Once we had crossed the stage, in one direction we were to wander back in the other, leave the stage and be done for the night. Not too taxing, except that having crossed the stage in one direction Peanuts was ready to head for the barn. Spotting the crimson curtain that framed the stage he would leap for it, hanging on with all his considerable might while screaming monkey epithets at me.

Opening night involved a minute or so of unplanned drama as I sought to pry him down from the curtain.

Once I was clued in to his plan I devised a plan of my own: shorten his leash as we approached the curtain so that he couldn't reach it. At the next performance, when he attempted his ad-lib, he was brought up short in mid-leap. As he began falling to the floor, Peanuts grabbed my leg to break his fall. When I reached down to put him back on my shoulder, he bit me with particular rage.

Not wanting to show a theatre-full of strangers that he had gotten the best of me, I endured the bite and we sauntered off the stage with him wrapped around my forearm, teeth in my skin and tears in my eyes.

Once we had finished our stroll, Peanuts and I would wait in the Green Room for the play to end, take our bows with the rest of the cast, and then hurry off to WTVN to prepare for the evening's broadcast. It was by now late winter or early spring—in Columbus there's little to choose between them—so Peanuts would make the trip beneath my overcoat, pressed against the warmth of my chest.

One night I drove downtown, parked, and entered the Buckeye Federal building as I routinely did. Less routinely, Peanuts did not poke his head out of the V above my coat buttons as was his custom. I figured he must be asleep and so did nothing to waken him. Entering the studio I stopped to greet Gene Fullen, who was then on-air. Gene was an all-purpose employee of Taft Broadcasting, owners of WTVN, and was heard regularly on both their radio and television outlets in Columbus. Gene had a rubbery face and a dry wit that made him a natural for local television in its infancy, and he appeared on his own TV show featuring live performances by local musical groups, as well as interviews with performing and recording celebrities on promotional tours. He was also the host of *Bowling For Dollars* and appeared regularly on *The Sally Flowers Show*. On radio, Gene's wit was best on display while riding herd on a bunch of used car salesmen hawking their wares during Saturday morning's perennial *Byers Bandwagon*. This night he was just another disc jockey filling the hours until the eleven o'clock news—what broadcasters call "feeding the monster."

I waited for Gene to finish his introduction of a record and close his mic, then began to exchange the usual remarks one makes on greeting a co-worker. A few seconds of this was enough to awaken Peanuts, who promptly thrust his head out of my coat. Blinking once or twice in the bright lights of the studio, he unexpectedly tore himself from beneath my coat and vaulted into the space before me. I watched in horror as his descent brought him down breathtakingly close to the turntable whose 45-rpm disc, at that moment, was the only thing driving WTVN's 5,000 watts of radiated power. Somehow he missed landing on the turntable itself, but while steadying himself next to the rotating surface, his tail barely flicked the pickup arm. Counterbalanced by weights so as to be feather-light in its contact with vinyl, the pickup arm responded to its brush with Peanut's tail by rising slowly off the record, thereby plunging the station into abrupt silence. The arm continued to ascend for perhaps three seconds, then took another three seconds to retrace its route back to the surface of the record, coming to rest in the exact spot where it had left.

As the music resumed, I dared to look Gene in the face. With his trademark scowl of amazement at the depths to which the human soul can descend, and convinced, I'm sure, that this was

merely another in a long series of elaborate stunts to break him
up on-air, he silently shoveled his personal stash of records into
the small valise that he always carried and walked out of the
studio, departing with the dignity of one who has again triumphed
over the philistines. The record, carefully timed to end at exactly
11 p.m., this night ran six seconds long.

[2] United States Pioneer Broadcast Service Stations, Thomas H. White,
January 1, 2005

ART BECOMES LIFE...
OR SOMETHING LIKE IT

Chapter five

A 45-RPM RECORD (at left). Broadcasters of the last century measured their lives by the two-and-a-half minutes of music each record provided.

In due course, Peanuts and I parted company. Call it irreconcilable differences. I wanted a soft and furry companion and he wanted to leave teeth marks on every part of my body. One day Ladylove and I drove Peanuts to the Columbus Zoo where, following a physical, he was inducted into an army of monkeys who delighted children (and frequently embarrassed their parents) while living lives of comparative freedom on an outdoor monkey island. A few years later I read that several monkeys had escaped from the island and taken to the trees that ringed the zoo. I haven't the least doubt who led the insurrection.

Once again the jungle drums beat out their message of hope for permanent employment, and I responded by arranging to audition for staff announcer at WBNS-TV. The position I auditioned for was part-time, as were my previous two employments, but I lived in the hope that I would be so good at my calling that a full-time position would be created for me, this despite the fact that the station already had more full-time announcers than it required, as well as several other part-timers.

In the 1950s and early '60s, WBNS-TV was the champagne television service in Columbus. It was, and still is, affiliated with CBS, then the dominant TV network nationwide. It did, and still does, share ownership with WBNS Radio and *The Columbus Dispatch*. And it employed the top on-air directing and engineering talent in Columbus, locally producing fine children's shows; musical programs, including remote broadcasts of the Columbus Symphony Orchestra; homemaker, farm report, and outdoor adventure shows; as well as every station's stock in trade: news, sports, and weather.

In the days of which I write, a radio studio could be located some distance from its transmitter, the signal being carried from one to the other on a telephone line with little loss of quality. But because a television signal degrades quickly from studio to transmitter to antenna, most TV studios actually housed their transmitter on the premises, with the antenna located just outside the studio walls. WBNS-TV's antenna was an immense structural steel affair, broad and triangular at its base and tapering with architectural precision as it reached 1,035 feet into the sky. Halfway up, the station's call sign was announced in giant red neon letters. As I walked to the front door of the station for the audition, I couldn't help but catch sight of the antenna looming above me. As my eyes wandered up, my heart sank. This was the big time, and suddenly I wasn't a bit sure I was ready.

Curiously, I don't remember the audition, only that I was hired. My hours were all over the clock and changed weekly. Every Wednesday a single sheet of paper was left in my mail slot detailing the days and hours I was to work the following week. It was not uncommon to find two and even three shifts scheduled for a single day, with too much time separating them to recommend hanging around the studios, but not enough time to undertake anything meaningful anywhere else.

I knew that this was a common practice in telecasting, and that many announcers killed time between shifts at favorite watering holes, where they sometimes were joined by the time salesmen from their stations. I also knew that not all of them became alcoholics, but enough did to warn me away from this practice. Additionally, I was earning the same amount I had at WTVN and that barely provided for food, much less a bar tab.

Before leaving WTVN I approached program director Bob Adkins and asked if he would consider replacing me with a young man whom I had met at student-staffed WOIO and whose air voice, I thought, exactly suited the nighttime audience. Bob agreed, and the next day I was pleased to introduce Bob to Dan Morris. Bob listened to Dan and instantly offered him my nighttime shift. Dan had a long and distinguished career in local broadcasting, both as on-air talent and as management, the latter including stints as General Manager of WCOL Radio, General Manager and part owner of WBBY-FM, and Vice President Radio, Eastern Operations, for Nationwide Communications. Dan today is Vice President of Communications for Grange Insurance.

It may have been my very first day in the announce booth that I perpetrated one of the biggest cock-ups in station history. Let me begin by telling what should have happened. Ann Reider, a gracious and talented spokeswoman for Ohio Fuel Gas Company (later Columbia Gas of Ohio), much in the mold of Westinghouse's Betty Furness, was in the studio about to do a live commercial for the utility. The commercial would begin with a few seconds of film (black and white, of course) of a hand holding a spatula, hacking away at a buildup of ice in the freezer compartment of a refrigerator. Over this film Ann was to say, "Here is a lady with a frost problem." The director would then dissolve to Ann on the studio floor, who would complete the sixty-second live read. My only task was to precede this by announcing the station's call letters over what is called a sig, or signature, slide that visually displayed the same information.

Everything was rehearsed and ready. We were coming out of network, and I was standing at the microphone, waiting for the red light on top of the conductor's stand holding the announcer's book to flash on. In the instant that it did, my mind went blank. Clearly I was to do something, but I couldn't for the life of me remember what.

Before continuing, I must explain that, in those wonderful days before videotape, almost all local commercials were done live. They could be as simple as an announcer reading copy as a series of slides were displayed in sync with the script, or as elaborate as a two- or three-camera shoot with one or more live presenters standing amid theatre lighting. Simple or elaborate, all the copy for all the commercials was spirit-mastered in fuzzy blue ink, placed in three-ring binders and distributed to all parties who might have a hand in that day's production. Thus, the copy that Ann was about to read was also in the announcer's book directly below my part: "WBNS-TV."

As I stared dumbly at the red light and heard the director's prompt in my headphones, "Go! Go!," the only thing I could think to do was to read the copy in front of me. Not the call letters, which I somehow failed to see, but "Here is a lady with a frost problem." It may have been the first time those words were ever spoken over a sig slide.

At this point the director realized I was lost so he quickly called for the switcher to drop the sig and take the film that had been pre-rolled and was ready for air. Unfortunately, in the confusion, the audio man forgot that there was sound on the film, even though it was to run silent. With the pot open on the film's audio track, we heard the film announcer say, "Here is a lady with a frost problem." At this point the director screamed to drop everything else and go live to the studio where, on doing so, we discovered

Ann staring into the camera with a bewildered look on her face. Quickly recovering, Ann put on her warmest smile and began reading from the teleprompter in front of her: "Here is a lady with a frost problem."

In both radio and television, any departure from the log must be noted on a discrepancy report. As the director interviewed one person after another, trying to piece together what had gone so badly wrong, he concluded that there wasn't space enough on the form to describe the problem in detail and noted simply, "Gas Company spot began late," thereby assuring a make-good commercial for the sponsor without implicating the new kid.

It's common for a station as large and prestigious as WBNS-TV to develop a "sound," a certain way of approaching the spoken word that, although uttered by different voices with different tonal qualities, still maintains a sameness with regard to pacing and inflection. To help me acquire the WBNS sound, I was schooled at intervals by both the chief announcer, Joe Holbrook, and the evening news anchor, Bill Pepper. It was a sound I would eventually acquire and it has remained with me throughout my life, shaping the way I still approach industrial video narration and even the occasional commercial. It's not a bad sound—until you have to do it on camera. Then, since shaping the sound can un-shape your face while making it, only those who can make the noise and still look natural had a future in the business.

I worked hard at trying to marry the WBNS sound with a natural look on camera and never succeeded. I had, as the saying goes, a face made for radio. Additionally, I am both cursed and blessed with my mother's strange sense of humor, which is to say that there's no way of predicting in advance what will reduce me to helpless laughter. I was in the studio one afternoon to do a live Pennington Bread commercial. It was a two-camera shoot, with camera one close-up on an open loaf of Pennington, a few slices of bread on a plate and a glass of milk—what's called a glamour shot. Camera two had a medium shot of me. Open on one, dissolve to two, then back to camera one as I read the commercial from the teleprompter. Thirty seconds and done. Simple.

As the duty director switched to the studio, the floor director, Chuck White, brought his hand down sharply, first finger extended, and pointed to the lens of camera one, the wordless sign that we were live and I should begin talking. Unfortunately, Chuck misjudged his distance from the lens and, instead of pointing to it, he banged his finger into it, then quickly withdrew it in obvious pain. That was it. I spoke a few words, suppressed a snicker and then dissolved into gales of laughter. Thirty painful seconds later, without another intelligible word being spoken, we rejoined the network, and another sponsor received a make-good because of me.

Chuck White is a gifted singer and musician who charmed central Ohio children for years as the gentle voice of Mr. Tree on "Lucy's Toyshop." At this writing, Chuck is in his forty-eighth year with WBNS-TV, much of it spent as the station's Public Affairs Director.

Eventually my booth work began to improve, and while I was no longer scheduled for on-camera commercials, I was being assigned more and more hours of staff announcing. Compared with radio's frantic pace, a TV staff announcer in the 1950s had almost nothing to do. A typical afternoon, for example, mostly involved watching a succession of CBS soap operas. A minute or two before each program ended, you would enter the booth, rehearse the commercials that were to be read during the next break, and then wait for the network throwaway, "This is the CBS Television Network." At this point, and on the director's cue through your headphones, you first identified the station, then read one thirty-second commercial and then another. As you read, it was the director's task to change slides or roll film as required to provide the visual component to the script. Seventy seconds after it began you were finished for the next twenty-eight minutes, fifty seconds. Note the commercials' start and stop times in the log, initial your entries, and pull up a chair for "As the World Turns."

As noted earlier, too much free time invites mischief, and local TV studios were not exempt. I watched in amusement one night as full-time announcer Don Riggs raced to finish reading a commercial on-air before the copy he was reading from disappeared. Dressed in a Shell Oil service station uniform, Don began the sixty-second spot reading from copy typed in large letters on yellow teleprompter paper that was taped to a tall, thin piece of Masonite board held just off camera. As he read, someone sneaked up behind the floor director holding the copy and set fire to the bottom of the paper. As Don read down the page, the fire burned up, and at some point before the end of the commercial Don was ad-libbing the final few sentences. To his credit, Don's dilemma would have gone unnoticed by a viewer at home.

Don's revenge, when it came, inevitably involved some innocents, one of whom was me. Coming out of the network at 10:59 p.m. there were likely to be three announcers in the tiny announce booth. The eleven o'clock break and the minutes on either side of it was one of two "money times" of the day, and the station wanted to put on its finest dress. One announcer would give the station's call letters and then read the first 30-second commercial, the second would read the second commercial, and the third was on hand to announce the open to the eleven o'clock news.

Jammed so tightly that you had to hold your arms together in front of you to avoid "touching," the most you could hope was to be assigned to read the first commercial, which would allow you to get out of the booth as quickly as possible.

On the night of Don's revenge there were three of us packed sardine-style into the booth, waiting for the network throwaway to begin our reads. With probably less than thirty seconds to the cue, the door to the booth was suddenly pulled open and Don somehow managed to insert himself among us. But only for a moment; just long enough to deliver the longest and most malevolently redolent flatulence in the history of the world. He then hopped back to the safety of the outside world before throwing his considerable weight against the handle of the door, pinning us all in our sulfurous tomb. Our eyes stung, our throats burned, and we thought the darkest of thoughts, but we also managed to pull off the break with no make-goods.

As I slowly improved, I began to take a fierce pride in completing a shift without a single stumble or misspoken word. And, of course, without being written up in the discrepancy report. One notable exception took place at a time when, fortunately, there were very few awake to hear it. A likeable young man on the floor crew was getting married and his bachelor party was planned for a Saturday night before I was scheduled for Sunday morning sign-on. While I was opposed to paying for beer, I was not averse to drinking someone else's and so consumed more than a few during the course of the evening.

Not wanting to risk oversleeping in my room at the fraternity house I drove to the station, let myself in the security door, and curled up on one of the desks in the newsroom, first posting a note on the control room door asking the engineers to wake me before sign-on. I had, it seemed, hardly gotten to sleep when a hand was shaking me, telling me it was time to get up.

I stumbled to the announce booth in time to read the sign-on announcement, after which the station played a film of flags flying, tanks rumbling, and jets screaming overhead, all to the strains of the National Anthem. Now, in those distant days, before the government largely relieved them of the responsibility, every radio and TV station in the country had to devote so much time each week to public service announcements—unpaid advertisements that promoted the general community welfare. While there was a mandate to make public service announcements (PSAs), there was no stipulation when they had to be broadcast, and Sunday morning sign-on was a chance to get a half-dozen or so out of the way when commercial time was not in demand. Ignoring the pounding in my head and the fur on my tongue, I launched into the first PSA and completed it without incident. Same with the second, the third, and so on. Finally, it was near the top of the hour. All that remained before going to the first pre-recorded program of the morning was to give the call letters, followed by a single-sentence plug for the Columbus Zoo—one more PSA credit for the station. Filled with confidence that I was the master of my lingering inebriation I said, "WBNS-TV. This Sunday, get the whole family together and zizit the Voo."

Even the considerable soundproofing that enveloped the announce booth was insufficient to screen out the howls of laughter from the director and engineers on duty. On emerging from the booth one of the engineers conferred on me a nickname that was to last well beyond the final few months of my employment with Channel 10, extending to many visits I made to the station as I began my 36-year career in advertising. He called me Old Polio Tongue. I guess I wasn't ready, after all.

Working at WBNS-TV introduced me to one of the most re-markable men I ever met: Marvin Fishman, aka Bob Marvin, aka Flippo, King of the Clowns. Bob began working at the station after serving with the Army in Korea, followed by studies at Ohio State beginning with optometry, then journalism, and finally music. While playing saxophone with a group appearing at Columbus' old Neil House Hotel, he was heard by a Channel 10 producer who offered him a job singing and appearing in sketches on the station's morning show. In 1952, the J. Walter Thompson ad agency asked WBNS-TV to produce a clown show for children for its client, the Ward Baking Company.

When a circus clown, who had accepted the role, later thought better of it and turned it down, Bob auditioned, won the part, and set out on a career that was to make him arguably the city's most recognizable and best-loved TV personality for more than 30 years. He was also the most unflinchingly honest and direct person I knew.

Bob didn't just play Flippo, he became Flippo out of a mixture of greasepaint and chutzpah. Mild-mannered and even serious in off-set conversation, Bob worked each day to become the dart-tongued wise guy in all of us who found a laugh within, or a great visual take at the end of almost everything he said. Bob spurned easy, pie-in-the-face comedy. His humor sprang from a quick wit, a musician's sense of the hip, and razor sharp timing. It could even be self-deprecating. You didn't laugh at him but with him.

I would watch each day as the transformation began about an hour before show time. Sitting in his t-shirt before the mirror in the men's dressing room, Bob began to disappear beneath a layer of Max Factor Clown White that extended from his hairline to the base of his throat and covered both his upper and lower eyelids. Next came the meticulously hand-painted and oversized red mouth. At this point a few zingers would be directed at his audience of one as Flippo began to replace Bob in his skin. Now a different artist's brush would be used to outline the mouth with a fine black line, then turned to highlighting the areas around the eyes, with three exclamation marks extending below the eyes and one up, ending above the brow line.

One-liners began to flow with rapid-fire precision as the final touch to his face—a bulbous red plastic nose—was spirit-gummed into place. His clown suit was a rich blue—a color deemed friendly by both the black-and-white TV cameras of the day and the early color cameras that replaced them. There was a large red collar at the throat and the suit was covered with white pompoms. The last part of the costume was a floppy blue hat with red trim, from the edges of which white yarn extended downward suggesting a fright wig barely contained. By the time the hat was in place, the theme song for *The Early Show* was playing and the floor crew, technicians, and director were praying that Flippo was on his way into the studio. He never missed a cue.

I occasionally got to announce around *The Early Show*, a two-hour afternoon movie liberally in-cut with commercial breaks that showcased Flippo's extraordinary gift for improvisation as he

Flippo, King of the Clowns

turned sponsors' sixty-second commercials into two- and three-minute comedy sketches.

The movie, ostensibly the reason for watching *The Early Show*, was a) usually old and not very good to begin with; b) disemboweled by film editors of any of its subplots to make room for the commercial breaks; and c) frequently run without airing as a succession of directors tried valiantly to keep the show on time and to have at least an ending of the movie for the viewers to see—the summation of a plot they probably never got to watch develop in the first place.

To my knowledge, no one ever complained about the movie.

Bob was a money machine for WBNS-TV. Sponsors not only stood in line to advertise on his show, they were also eager to use "the Clown" at all manner of public appearances: ground breakings, ribbon cuttings, grand openings, new model year auto introductions, community service, and school events—a list almost without end. What portion of this income the station kept and what it shared with Bob were never discussed in my presence, but I sensed Bob didn't think it entirely fair. The station did buy Flippo an Isetta, BMW's micro car nicknamed the "rolling egg," and painted it to identify the occupant as its premiere talent. Seeing the Isetta pull up at an event was enough to assure maximum turnout of all ages, genders, and socioeconomic strata, to say nothing of gladdening the organizer's heart.

Bob and I worked most closely together after I left WBNS-TV and the station offered him an additional one-hour live show on Saturday mornings. Unlike *The Early Show*, this hour was to be all Flippo with no movie to compete for the viewer's attention. It was also to be scripted. I was flattered when Bob asked me if I would join him as co-writer of the show and we began working evenings in his home. Sitting in a room illuminated only by the dancing light from his saltwater aquarium, we bounced ideas and dialog off each other until neither of us could stay awake. He would then take one piece of the script to complete, and I would take the other. When the writing for the week's show was done, Bob would perform the final edit, and it would be sent off to be loaded on teleprompters.

I have very few memories of the actual shows: a live parrot that was supposed to sit on his shoulder but took off just before airtime to roost in the light grid and was never seen on camera; the actress, Zada van Dorn as Mrs. Rinkydoo, skillfully playing Flippo's friend or foil as the plot required. Mostly I remember that the show lasted just enough weeks to demonstrate that Bob's genius was too large to be contained by a scripted format and that it disappeared as quickly as it had arrived.

The very day I began writing these graphs about Bob, he passed away at the age of seventy-nine, though I didn't learn of his death until a day or two later because I was traveling. I wish I could have said goodbye.

Summer of 1959 marked the high water of my carefree bachelor life. I was dating not one, but two new Ladyloves. One, ironically and accidentally, was the boss's daughter. And when I say the boss, I mean the big boss—capo di capo. I had met her two years before as a high school senior on a blind date in Toledo. When I moved to Columbus I would call her from time to time when there was a likelihood that she was home from her studies at Bryn Mawr.

Now, a typical summer Sunday would have me signing on her father's TV station a few minutes before 6 a.m. and working until 10:30 a.m., after which I'd return to the fraternity house to shower, shave and dress, then drive to her home in the fashionable suburb of Bexley. Afternoons were spent in and alongside the family pool, drinking her father's Michelob, and being watched with some care by either her mother or brother. The family had plans for their daughter that clearly didn't involve a part-time TV announcer who warmed Dinty Moore corned beef hash in a popcorn popper and called it supper. I saw her father maybe twice in a summer of Sundays and believe he spoke half as many words to me. As the afternoons wore down, I would suit up and return to the station, announcing around and past *The Ed Sullivan Show* until sign-off.

I met the other Ladylove when her family came to the TV station for a visit, and I was asked to give them the nickel tour. Her father was a successful audiologist in Columbus, and his idea of a great afternoon was remarkably similar to my own: take his boat to the Scioto River and see how much waterskiing you could get in before sunset—or until your schedule summoned you back to the station.

The hearing aid man had two daughters, one of whom was warm and generous, and the two of us dated, mostly in the company of her family, until she returned to school and I read my final sign-off at WBNS-TV.

At long last, one of the full-time jobs that I had been promised "when there's a position open" became available, and I quickly signed with WRFD Radio. Too quickly, as I would later come to believe.

But in the first heady months of new employment with a regular paycheck in a predictable amount, I remember feeling that life didn't get any better than this. As if to underscore the point, I soon made another of the many friendships that would extend through all my years in advertising to the present day.

Promotion was the name of the game in a highly competitive radio market, and WRFD played to win. The entire air staff was expected to involve themselves in as many community activities as possible, bringing needed attention and, it was hoped, new listeners to the station.

At different times I remember riding the Junior Chamber of Commerce dunking chair at the Ohio State Fair dressed in an old fashioned, knee-length swimming suit; serving as master of ceremonies at a 1960 Nixon campaign rally featuring movie actress Irene Dunne and Minnesota congressman Walter Judd; and attending countless area sock hops during which I played music for the teens that would never have been allowed on our conservative station.

The first such activity I was directed to by WRFD's promotion department was a go-cart race at a local speedway. One heat of the evening's races was to feature area broadcasters driving the carts with the winner's share going to charity. The promoters called it the Oil Can Derby, and I was eager to take my turn at the wheel.

The Powell Motor Speedway was nothing but a dirt oval ringed with barely adequate lighting, one of seemingly hundreds you see beneath you on a summer's flight to almost anywhere in America. Given maybe two minutes of instruction in the fine points of go-cart racing, I soon found myself at the starting line with five other drivers. When the flag dropped, I shoved the throttle forward and fell into column behind the leader. Over the course of however many laps constituted a heat, I managed to work my way into the lead. Clattering to the finish line, I was reviewing locations where I might display the small winner's trophy to its best advantage when I looked to my right and saw another driver and cart slowly stealing my lead. To win, he would have to make me come off my pace, and this he did by simply angling his cart into mine. A few yards from the checkered flag I braked to avoid a collision, and the other driver sailed across the finish line in front of me.

An inauspicious beginning to what was to become a fast friendship, I climbed out of my cart and stoically grasped the hand of the tall, skinny, grinning winner. His name, I learned, was Bill Hamilton, and from that moment Bill and I became good friends as well as career competitors. For the rest of my years in broadcasting, Bill and I would frequently go head-to-head, seeking to win or retain the same job. True to our go-cart experience, Bill usually came out ahead.

When I married, Bill was a frequent bachelor guest in our home. When our daughter Kathy was born, Bill was our very first baby sitter. When we finally worked together at the same station,

Bill would hang around until I finished my shift and then we'd
have breakfast together about 1:30 in the morning. And when
Bill finally left broadcasting to become one of the most successful
freelance announcers in the Midwest, it was my happy task to em-
ploy him on many occasions to voice commercials and industrial
videos for several of my clients. As I write this, I have asked Bill
to appear on a panel with radio veterans remembering their years
in broadcasting, which will air on a local public radio station. As I
expected, Bill readily agreed.

Another activity during those first few months at WRFD may
just have provided the consummate example of life imitating art.
John Metzger was a writer-producer for what was then Columbus'
largest advertising agency, Byer and Bowman. A staunch Ohio State
alumnus, John had agreed to write and direct an audio recording that would highlight Ohio State's 1959-60 school year. Filled
with snippets of recordings of football and basketball broadcasts;
marching band performances; concerts by various glee clubs and
choirs; iconic campus sounds, including the distinctive Orton Hall
chimes; and held together by narration, the recording was to be
pressed into 45-rpm records and placed into sleeves glued to the
inside back cover of the 1960 Ohio State yearbook, *Makio*. Titled
"This is Ohio State 1960," the record was distributed that year as
widely as the yearbook itself, traveling with graduating seniors and
other students throughout much of the world.

John asked me if I would be one of two narrators on the recording, and I readily agreed. For the woman's voice he recruited
Jodi Sanderson, a senior at Ohio State who had already secured
postgraduate employment with Voice of America. I don't recall
having met Jodi or John before we collaborated on this project,

and I never saw or heard from Jodi again, although John and I later worked together for a brief time in the same advertising agency.

As with most "opportunities" in broadcasting, there would be no pay for my services.

John began writing in the fall of 1959 and we recorded the narration one evening in the early spring of 1960. To make the recording, I offered John the use of the studios at WRFD, a fact of which management may still be unaware. One aspect of my life in those days that I take no pride in was that I could rationalize using a studio for my own purposes as something somehow owed to me because of some real or imagined slight. Had I asked management if I could have used the studio for this purpose, I'm sure they would have said yes. Not asking was my childish bid at having things my own way.

When the narration was complete, John took the tape with him to be built into the mix of other sounds that would make up the final recording. I subsequently received a copy of the finished record with a note of thanks from John and, within months, had forgotten completely about it.

Nine years later, while reading a publication called *The University Forum*, I came across a review by Richard Brown of Philip Roth's National Book Award-winning novella, *Goodbye, Columbus*, published in 1959. In the article I was astonished to realize that the title of Roth's book refers to "an (Ohio State) graduation record which Ron Patimkin calls his Columbus record and which he loves dearly."

From Roth's book: "And finally there came a Voice, bowel-deep and historic, the kind one associates with the documentaries about the rise of Fascism. The place, the banks of the Olentangy. The event, Homecoming Game, 1956. The opponent, the ever dangerous Illini."

From Metzger's script for the actual recording: "It was a great day for all as the battling Bucks trounced Purdue, fifteen to nothing, and we heard the Victory Bell ringing again."

Roth had invented a record that extolled life at Ohio State as a literary device to advance the storyline of a novella that was published in the same year that Johnny Metzger was writing a script for a record that extolled life at Ohio State to accompany an otherwise mute yearbook.

I'm not sure the odds on that kind of coincidence can be calculated.

Sadly, Roth does neither Columbus nor Ohio State any favors in his book, associating them, according to Brown, "with everything that is fake, stupid, reprehensible and obnoxious in middle class American life." Here is the conclusion of the recording from Roth's novella:

"We offer ourselves to you, then, world, and come at you in search of life. And to you, Ohio State, to you, Columbus, we say thank you, thank you and goodbye. We will miss you, in the fall, in the winter, in the spring, but some day we shall return. Till then, goodbye, Ohio State, goodbye red and white, goodbye, Columbus. Goodbye, Columbus. Goodbye."

The closing text of the actual recording is different from Roth's principally in its specific references to life at Ohio State:

"Well, that's it, I guess. We'd better go pack. Couldn't resist one last look, though. What will we remember most? The TGIF's at Larry's? The thrill of the big game with its swarms of people? The halftime show? Or the sudden stillness of a Wednesday morning (when taps are played on the Oval in memory of former students who lost their lives in our nation's wars). Or will it be the pizzas at Romeo's? Or the hamburgers at Charbert's? Calling home for more dough? Or Mirror Lake, landmark of laughter, of friendship and merriment? Well, I don't know. But I do know that we'll be back. After all, we'll always think of 15th and High as the center of the universe. And let's face it, no one ever really leaves Ohio State. And once you've had the four-year Buckeye treatment, who wants to? Not I."

It's fun to reflect on the incredible similarities between these independent inventions, and sad to consider how badly wide of the mark are Roth's observations about my adopted city of Columbus. Routinely voted among the top cities in America for its quality of life and its environment, Columbus is warm and welcoming to newcomers, and makes minimal distinctions based on where you live or went to school. And if Columbus is passionate about its football Buckeyes, I'm at a loss to understand how this is somehow less acceptable than being a Yankees or a Red Sox fan.

Well, it's his book so he gets to tell it his way. But Mr. Roth, there's just one thing: It's scarlet and gray, you weenie, not "red and white."

art becomes life... or something like it

State Prison of Southern Michigan
OPERATION LEAKY ARM
May it be known from this day forth

KEN KELLER

has been convicted of the crime of aiding and abetting O. L. A. and is hereby sentenced to a term of LIFE as an HONORARY CONVICT.

Gordon Fuller — Executive Director

Al Fist Top Daly — Executive Sec'y

№ 286

Voice of OPERATION LEAKY ARM

MY FIRST INTERVIEW with George Shearing in the studios of WRFD.

Technically, WRFD was not a Columbus radio station, though it competed in that market. Begun by the Ohio Farm Bureau Federation and during my tenure owned and operated by Nationwide Insurance, WRFD was located in a handsome single story brick building on a gentle rise of pasture land north of the Columbus bedroom community of Worthington. Its two studios were encircled by a richly carpeted hallway whose walls were adorned by a succession of Currier and Ives lithographs. A display of antique radio receivers greeted visitors in the lobby.

Though rural in its origins, as well as in the content of its early morning and noon programs, WRFD tried hard to be a force in the Columbus market. But with call letters chosen to remind listeners that it specialized in Rural Farm Delivery, the station was seldom considered seriously by media buyers seeking to reach the large and affluent Columbus urban market. Of several stations then owned by Columbus-based Nationwide Insurance, it was the only one that all the many vice presidents of the parent company could listen to, form opinions about, and seek to influence with a local telephone call. Life could not have been easy for station manager Joe Bradshaw.

WRFD was, and is, a "daytimer"—that is, it is required by the Federal Communications Commission to sign on at daybreak and to sign off at dusk. An AM radio station's signal travels farther at night than during the day because ionospheric reflection—the tendency of signals to bounce off the ionosphere to far distant locations—is increased at night.

Signing off at dusk kept WRFD's 5,000 watt signal from interfering with WCBS Radio's 50,000 watt signal screaming west from New York City on the same frequency.

While working for a daytimer had the advantage of keeping my evenings free, the downside was that I was to be the station's "accordion." As our broadcast hours lengthened in the spring, because dusk came later and later, I was there to fill them with music. As they contracted in the fall, I was the one whom listeners would hear less and less until I all but disappeared from the air. During the "dark months" I was assigned to pre-record a host of commercials and program open-and-close announcements that would be used the following morning to provide another voice during those hours, as well as to undertake various feature projects—man-on-the-street interviews, etc.—that held no interest for me at all. As I was hired just as the dark months of 1959-60 were beginning, my career in broadcasting took a decided left turn.

The fact is WRFD and I were not a good fit from the start, for which I assume most of the blame. Staffed by men and women who came from a rural ethic, their stoic and, to me at least, humorless approach to the fine comedy of broadcasting made them difficult to understand. I was once sternly reprimanded for playing jazz legend Nina Simone's recording of George Gershwin's "I Loves You Porgy." The offending lyrics read: "I loves you Porgy / don't let him take me / don't let him handle me with his hot hands."

Ms. Simone, according to station manager Phil Sheridan, sounded "as if she were down on the floor, wiggling."

For management's part, my unfocussed energy, lack of personal discipline, and constant need to be doing something new made me impossible to admire. I was unhappy with the amount of airtime I was getting and took pains to make sure everyone around me knew it. Still, it took them two and a half years to get around to firing me, and that's time enough to have lived a few adventures worth retelling.

One such enterprise began in early December 1959 as I was scanning articles in the trade publication, *Broadcasting*. A small story near the bottom of a page contained an appeal from a fellow disc jockey. His name was Al "Flat Top" Daley and his "station" was a closed circuit network in the State Prison of Southern Michigan at Jackson. The story read, "If you want to brighten the darkest time of the year for the boys here and have an extra fifteen minutes to cut a tape, come ahead. Remember, no seasonal music as the boys are doing hard time anyhow just being away from their loved ones this time of year." Mr. Daly, I later learned, had contributed to being away from his "loved ones" by murdering his wife.

To the extent that WRFD could boast of having a star, it would have been our afternoon man, Bill Collins. Bill was well read and erudite, and he had a large and loyal following. I asked Bill if he would work with me in producing a half-hour radio program to assist Mr. Daly, who was readying all-night record shows for the inmates that would air the two eves before Christmas. A subsequent newspaper article on what followed said that Bill and I produced the program and sent it off to the prison. My memory of this event is incomplete, but I don't recall that Bill had a hand in the recording.

Nevertheless, the following March, Bill and I were both "indicted" for our services to the prison and made Honorary Convicts, numbers 286 (me) and 287. In this we joined such other famous "cons" as bandleader Ray Conniff (226), singer Kay Starr (277), actress Debbie Reynolds (177), and Columbia Records' legendary Mitch Miller (310). But Al "Flat Top" Daly (No. 77582) wasn't done with us yet.

Mr. Daly's principal "in-house" activity was organizing and directing a massive blood donor effort among his fellow inmates in order to preserve what was perhaps a self-given title, the World's Champion Blood Donors. Called "Operation Leaky Arm," or OLA, the effort did produce remarkable benefits. With fewer than 3,000 donors to draw from, OLA routinely supplied the Red Cross with 2,000-plus pints of blood. With each new drive, Mr. Daly sought to raise the bar, coaxing more and more of the precious red fluid from his pals through a well-developed public relations program, including radio appeals inside the institution and letters to editors and a growing list of supporters outside. He also published a single-page newsletter, *Here Comes Needles*.

For one such drive in 1960, Mr. Daly invited his Honorary Convicts in broadcasting to also become donors while promising a trophy to the radio station whose staff contributed the most blood in OLA's name. In for a penny, in for a pound, I now sought to enlist WRFD's staff in OLA's drive. I don't recall how many of us shed a pint for Flat Top; I know that it was more than just me and less than the entire staff. Whatever the number, it turned out that WRFD had donated the most blood, and I was invited to Jackson to pick up a trophy honoring our station as National Champions of the "Deejay Donor Duel."

A brief sidebar to this story: Since going to work for WRFD, I had become reacquainted with a former Ladylove, and our relationship quickly grew into a romance that by now extends to forty-eight years and counting. Mary and I had met at Ohio State at an ice skating party for pledges arranged by the active members of our respective fraternity and sorority. She had been paired for the evening with my fellow pledge Ron Taylor and I with a woman whose name escapes me. Coincidentally, she, herself, escaped me sometime during the course of the evening. Now, it was late and

I was driving the three of us back to campus, I in the front seat
of My Fair Lady and Ron and Mary in the back. We pulled up
in front of Bradley Hall, and Ron walked Mary to the door. As I
waited for him, I noted that the car adjacent to mine was similar
in almost every detail to my own, except for the couple in the
front seat whose bodies and faces were annealed to each other's.
I watched Ron begin walking back to my car and realized that he
was heading, not for MFL, but for the identical car on my right.
I leaned across the front seat and rolled down the window to get
his attention just in time to see Ron pull open the passenger door
of the wrong car and start to get in. As he did so, I heard him
exclaim, "Holy shit, Keller, let's get outta here, I have to piss like
a sonofabitch." In the glare of the car's overhead light, Ron now
confronted the angry face of the driver, momentarily detached
from his date's: "Ya got the wrong car, buddy." Ron shot out of the
car, mumbling an apology, and calling my name for directions to
the proper car. He was guided to it by peals of laughter issuing
through the open window.

A week or so later I was cleaning out the back seat of MFL
when I found a gray scarf that I didn't recognize. Stitched in the
corner was a tag with Mary's name. I called her at the dorm to tell
her I'd found her scarf and would come by to return it. We met,
talked, and agreed that we'd like to meet again.

Mary was cute, wise, and full of fun, and since neither of us
was interested in anything more than a friendship, we limited our
contact to the occasional movie and sometimes a meal, when one
or the other of us could afford them. A few months went by before
it occurred to us to kiss. Because I wasn't looking for romance,
it came as something of a surprise when I discovered it, and my

initial response was to run from it, first creating the requisite arguments that made separating both necessary and possible. Most of a year went by before we met again, and all the love and the loss that I had been feeling could find its true expression. When it was time to pick out a ring set for Mary, I mentioned the fact to Flippo (I never referred to Bob by any other name, nor was I alone in doing so). True friend that he was, he insisted that Mary and I should buy from his friend, Howard Johnson, owner of Johnson Jewelers. To make sure we got the deal he promised we would, Flippo asked us to pick him up on our way to the store. One of the happiest memories of my wedding year is the morning Flippo, kindly Mr. Johnson, Mary, and I stood together in a circle picking out the perfect ring.

For the trip to Jackson, I invited Mary to keep me company. I'm not sure what I thought Mary would do while I was in the prison accepting the award; what I hadn't guessed was that she would be admitted right along with me—no small test of her tendency toward claustrophobia.

Because of the ease with which I had exchanged letters, newsletters, broadcast recordings, membership cards, and once even a telephone call with Mr. Daly, my mental picture of his living arrangements had distinctly fuzzy edges. Now, of a sudden, those edges were in plain view, and they were sharp and stark. Leading away from the lobby area of the prison was a hallway framed in steel and stoppered at regular intervals by checkpoints and door-size turnstiles. I was made to empty my pockets into a manila envelope, Mary surrendered her purse, and we acquired a guide who would be with us for the remainder of our stay. More steel-ringed halls, more checkpoints, and we finally arrived at the very center of the prison. The area, as best I remember all these years since, was round and open and extended up several floors. A smaller raised area in the center of the first floor served as the guards' command post. Ringing the open area on the first floor were enclosed offices and meeting rooms, while the remaining floors had balconies with walkways that lead to the cells. While all the architectural details do not live in my memory, the color, for some reason, does. Everything was painted the same shade of pale green. Illuminated by banks of fluorescent lamps, whose natural blueness tended to soften the green paint even further, the effect was like being lost in a wilderness of pale green snow as viewed through the trunks of steel trees. Off to one side was a small room with a table, chairs, and a microphone, and to this our guide now pointed us.

I am reminded by the July 1961 issue of *Here Comes Needles* that Mary and I arrived during Mr. Daly's program "Blues, Ballads and Bop." I was interviewed and then presented with the station's trophy. I can see from the accompanying photograph that even my simple brown suit and tie constituted major overdressing. And without prompting I remember feeling well treated and secure, wanting very much to like the men about me and being upset with myself that I could not. What manner of choice, if that's what it was, accounted for the difference between my being able to get up from the table and leave the wilderness when the show was over and the other men having to remain behind? Faced with identical circumstances, what choices would I have made? On the long drive home I turned these questions over and over in my mind.

A road trip to Michigan's prison system notwithstanding, most of my off-premises work for WRFD involved interviewing celebrities passing through Columbus, and over a period of time I became rather good at it. The trick, I learned early on, was to let the interviewee say the things he or she needed to say, then find a thread to follow in their prepared answers and let it lead the two of you to the unprepared and therefore spontaneous. This can only happen when you understand and accept that you first need to be "used."

The only reason that you are granted access to a celebrity's time and attention is that you provide a conduit to an audience that needs to be informed of the celebrity's agenda, whether to sell a record, pitch a performance date or movie opening, or advance a cause. During the interview, and preliminary to revealing his or her agenda, the celebrity is on high alert, listening for cues that he or she can use to charm your listeners and make them receptive to the pitch that follows. As the interviewer, you also are on high alert, hoping to create a mood of such familiarity that your listeners are convinced that the two of you routinely dine in each other's homes, or at least stay in touch by telephone. It's a fine dance and, at its best, it's believable. By its very nature it's also superficial; until the moment you sit down to talk you've probably never met. But a celebrity is, before anything else, a person, with all the hopes and frustrations of everyone else you know. They push on doors marked pull, have stomach cramps while traveling, and worry about their children, or at least their incomes, with the best of us. But once their agendas have been attended to, if your interest is genuine and your questions on the mark, they're apt to connect with you at a very human level. And when it really goes well, they just might come home with you to dinner.

The first time this happened I was still living at the Phi Delt
house. I had interviewed a beautiful young American singer who
was appearing at Danny Deed's Maramor on East Broad Street and
who was in the process of setting the popular music world on its
ear with her recording of "Don't You Know." Della Reese was a
wonder: tall, slim, intelligent, with a voice like a French horn and
impeccable diction. As our interview ended, I suddenly found the
nerve to ask her if she would be my guest at the fraternity house
for dinner. To my astonishment, she agreed.

Late the next afternoon I picked her up at her hotel and we
drove to the house on Iuka Avenue. The evening meal required
the brothers to be in coat and tie, and places had been set at the
head table for my guest and me. As we entered the room there was
a slight stir that I naively attributed to the brothers' reaction to
being in such close proximity to our famous guest. But I gradually
realized this was not a happy, nor even a self-conscious stirring;
this was contained but undisguised resentment to the presence of a
black woman in this all-white, all-male dining room.

I felt my confusion growing and also my anger. Something
needed to be said, but I couldn't think of anything that wouldn't
make the situation worse. I needn't have been concerned. When,
at the end of the meal, I was asked by the president of the chapter
to introduce my guest, I said something lame about how we hoped
Ms. Reese might sing for her supper. With that, this elegant and
composed young woman rose to her feet and said, "Well, I'm not
going to sing for you, but I would like to make an observation. I
thank you for inviting me to your house for dinner, but as I look
around this room, I can't help noticing that if I wasn't famous, I

wouldn't be welcome here. And that makes me sad." With that, she sat down. I don't remember what happened next. I'm sure I returned her to her hotel, but I don't remember what, if anything, was said during the drive. I'm equally sure my face burned with embarrassment. What I am certain about is that I subsequently moved out of the fraternity house and have never returned. A year or so later I asked Mr. Johnson if he would pry the small ruby and diamond chips from my fraternity pin and reset them in a ring for Mary.

Another guest who came to dinner, or at least to dessert and coffee, was William Tabbert. Bill's name may not be familiar to today's reader, but the characters he created and the songs he introduced during his distinguished stage career are legendary. On April 7, 1949, Bill became part of Broadway history, appearing opposite Ezio Pinza and Mary Martin in the Broadway premiere of Rogers and Hammerstein's *South Pacific*. In the role of Lt. Cable, Bill introduced the quintessential Broadway love song "Younger than Springtime," and later in the same show, the supremely ironic "You've Got to be Taught."

Six years later Bill teamed up with Pinza once again, creating the role of Marius in the Broadway premiere of *Fanny,* which also starred Walter Slezak and a youthful Florence Henderson in the title role. As a young man torn between his love for Fanny and his passion for the sea, Marius sings the haunting "Restless Heart" and later the title song itself. Bill was one of several artists who came together under the baton of Maestro Evan Whallon to perform an evening of Broadway favorites with the Columbus Symphony Orchestra.

I caught up with Bill one afternoon during rehearsal, and shortly after beginning the interview I realized that his career, as well as his wonderfully open personality, would easily overflow the half-dozen minutes of conversation I required. I asked Bill if he would accompany me to WOSU Radio, which he did, and there I introduced him to its music director, Fred Calland, later National Public Radio's first music producer.

Fred's knowledge of music of all sorts, Broadway included, was encyclopedic, and he quickly abandoned whatever else he was doing to sit down and begin an extended interview with Bill. Every discussion point seemed to have its resolution in one of Bill's cast recordings, and I remember best Fred asking him if he ever thought of Pinza, who had died shortly before. Bill's eyes welled with tears as he began to answer, and after a few false starts, settled for "I think of him every day of my life." In the finished production of the half-hour interview, this quiet statement led directly to a recording of the duet from *Fanny*, "I Like You," which begins with Marius singing to his father, Panisse, played by Pinza, "I like you / Like you very much / More than I could ever show." It was a grand moment in radio.

When rehearsal finally ended that evening, I invited Bill back to our apartment before returning him to his hotel. Still eager to remember his years on Broadway, Bill told Mary and me a story about *South Pacific* rehearsals. "At a certain point in the show," Bill said, "we all knew this love song would be sung. Only it hadn't been written yet. Day after day, we'd get to that point in rehearsal and the director, Josh Logan, would say, 'OK, skip the song and continue.' Finally, one day, Oscar and Dick sat down at this battered rehearsal piano and, with the cast in a circle around them, Dick played and Oscar sang 'Younger than Springtime.' When they were finished, no one could speak for a moment. Finally, Dick's valet, who was also there, leaned over to me and said, 'You know, Mr. Bill, some man sure must love some woman to write a song like that.' I couldn't have agreed more."

One interview I conducted might have led to a deeper personal relationship if I hadn't gotten both of us lost in the process. As with many failed ideas, it seemed a good one at the time. Nat Greenberg was the general manager of the Columbus Symphony Orchestra and so was responsible for transporting visiting guest artists from the airport to their hotel and back, as well as from their hotel to the concert hall for rehearsals and performances. I told Nat that I would be happy to provide the airport-to-hotel-and-back legs of the journey in exchange for the opportunity to interview the orchestra's guests on their arrival, and he quickly agreed. Most of the artists I drove were amenable to a brief interview once they were settled in their hotel, but some said they were simply too tired from their travel and wanted to rest.

To improve my chances of getting an interview, I jury-rigged a device to the dashboard of my car that would hold a microphone, its cord falling downward to a battery-powered tape recorder that I slid under the driver's seat. To begin the interview, I simply brought out the recorder, pressed the right combination of levers, and began talking. I tried out the device while driving around a block not far from my residence and it seemed to work pretty well. There was a little ambient traffic noise but only enough to suggest that the recording was made on location and not in a studio. I thought it added to the immediacy of the event.

The first artist on whom I tried this new technique was the distinguished American composer Aaron Copland, who was to conduct an evening of his own works with the orchestra. When I explained what I intended, Maestro Copland was dubious but willing, and once his luggage was in the trunk and we were away from the airport, I brought out the recorder, pushed the right levers and began talking. Things seemed to be going well until I realized that I was hopelessly lost. Today's commute from the airport to downtown Columbus is over a well-marked, six-lane divided highway. In those days it was through city streets. Owing partly to my still being new to Columbus, and partly to my having a truly terrible sense of direction, I—that is, we—were hopelessly lost in the tangle of streets that is the suburb of Bexley.

Distracted as I was with our predicament, the interview quickly ground to a halt. Just as quickly, I'm sure, my passenger began assessing the possibility that he was being kidnapped by a crazy person.

I quickly put away the recorder, picked a direction at random and began driving in a straight line in the hope of eventually finding something that looked familiar. It took a while but I finally did intersect a street that I knew, not all that far from the airport where we began. I completed the delivery in embarrassed silence, the more so when Nat asked me to also provide Maestro Copland with transportation to and from rehearsals and performances. We saw each other several times over the next three days, and he never failed to greet me with a smile—wary, perhaps, but still a smile.

I never again attempted the rolling interview trick, though I did use a variation of it in making an extended recording with violin virtuoso Yehudi Menuhin. Marsha and Doug Kohler owned a lovely house in Bexley, and by prearrangement with them, I converted their dining room into a temporary recording studio. After picking Mr. Menuhin and his wife up at the airport, we simply stopped at the Kohlers on our way into town and made a fine recording of Mr. Menuhin that was later broadcast, as well as pressed into flexible sound sheets, all in support of the orchestra's annual fund drive.

The whole thing went very well, and I didn't get a bit lost.

Only two of my interview tapes from that era still exist, one with a comedienne who was just beginning her career, and the other with a comedian who helped to write the history of network radio. Two things strike me about these tapes after listening to

Following the aborted interview: from left, Columbus Symphony Orchestra Music Director Evan Whallon, your chagrinned correspondent, and Aaron Copland.

them for the first time in almost forty years. One is the painfully slow and studied way that I framed my questions, and the other is the richness and depth of the answers I received.

Phyllis Diller, on how she created her persona: "I have tried to put into what I do all of the classic humor and funny techniques that have been used by everybody who has ever done humor. I go clear back to the court jester for my stance. I crouch and lean over and stick my head forward, as the old hunchback did to make the king laugh. But you see, Ken, my material is new. I'm a gagster. I do one-liners. Now, the new group that are really in the ascendancy—Bob Newhart, Shelley Berman, Elaine May, and Mike Nichols—they don't use a lot of one-liners. But my entire act is constructed of nothing but them." Though the point hardly needs proving, the *Guinness Book of World Records* attests that in her prime, Ms. Diller could deliver twelve punch lines per minute.

Edgar Bergen talked with me on the history and art of ventriloquism: "It goes back 200, 300 years before Christ. It was practiced by the Greeks and the Chinese. But I had to come up with my own explanation, because what I could read was inconsistent. Some would say it was a complete optical illusion, others would say it was a rare gift. So I've come up with my own definition. I say ventriloquism is voice diffusion. It is accomplished by putting pressure on the vocal cords, and it seems to diffuse the voice so you can't tell where it's coming from. And it's more than an optical illusion, because it's practiced by animals. The chickadee is an excellent ventriloquist, and I was fooled beautifully by a chickadee. And I've fooled dogs many times in homes. So it's not a question of holding your lips and making the puppet's mouth move. There's more to it than that, because the dog is not watching your lips."

"A simple demonstration of it all is, for example, Charlie's voice is up here and he talks up about here, like that, but it's not truly ventriloquism until I do that and now it becomes ventriloquism in a ventriloquial voice. 'Hello, Bergen.' 'Hello, Charlie.' 'Hello, hello.'"

And there, for just a moment, in a room in a hotel that no longer exists, Charlie McCarthy came to life for me. I'd made good on my boyhood promise; I'd found where one of my radio heroes lived.

At another point in the interview I asked Mr. Bergen if he had a favorite among his "mahogany children." He replied, "Well, I think I'm like the old mother hen, or the mother of the family: I try to distribute my love equally. However, Mortimer (Snerd) is—Charlie can stand on his own, but Mortimer needs a little more love than Charlie, and I think there's something very charming about Mortimer, cause he knows he's stupid, and this is great wisdom, to know you're not smart."

The night I interviewed Ms. Diller was snowy and late, and having learned the Ampex tape recorder's penchant for running off-speed when it was cold, I was letting it warm up in record mode while we chatted. As the tape begins, Ms. Diller, remembering an earlier interview we did together, remarks, "Ho, ho, ho, ho, Ken Keller. When Sherry (first husband, Sherwood Diller) told me that you had called, I said, 'The Highbrow.' (Signature laugh) I shall always think of you as The Highbrow." It was such a charming piece of intimacy that I left it in the final edit.

Occasionally I would participate in "cattle call" interviews, during which ten or twelve interviewers would take turns asking questions of a celebrity. I once interviewed Bob Hope in this fashion at the foot of the steps leading down from the plane that had brought him to Columbus for a concert date at Ohio State. Before it was my turn to ask a question, and without my being aware of it, the wind whipping around the plane blew the tape off the capstan of my recorder so that from that point on no recording was being made. I discovered the problem as I was packing up to leave. In desperation I called Bill Teague at WBNS Radio. Bill was the dean of radio field reporters and, being the professional that he was, had recorded the entire interview session, including my questions and Mr. Hope's answers. When he learned of my problem, Bill generously agreed to share his tape with me. But by the time I had driven into town to pick up the tape, driven back to our suburban studio and edited it for broadcast, we were the last station to air an interview—another black mark in the book WRFD was beginning to keep on me.

Another cattle call interview was with Red Skelton in the main studio of WBNS-TV, my old stomping ground. CBS had sent Mr. Skelton out to promote his new season on the network. When it was my turn to ask a question, I wondered what his reaction was to the equation usually attributed to Mel Brooks that "comedy equals tragedy plus time." Mr. Skelton said he thought this was a useful definition and immediately launched into an impromptu story to illustrate it. In the story, old Joe has died and his coffin is being transported to the cemetery in the back of a horse-drawn hearse. As the team of horses picks its way up the rutted road leading to the cemetery, the door on the back of the hearse suddenly swings open, the coffin falls out and splits wide apart, leaving poor old Joe in the dust. The next day, people are talking about what happened. "Did you hear about old Joe?" "Yes, it's awful." "Terrible, just terrible." A couple of years later these same people are talking. "Remember what happened to old Joe?" "Yeah." "Pretty funny, huh?" "Funniest thing I ever saw." These words, combined with Mr. Skelton's consummate skill at characterization, made for a wonderful comedic moment. Because the interview was telecast live, we were told not to bring recording devices with us to the studio. Accordingly, WBNS-TV's audience was treated to this delightful and impromptu moment while my audience was not.

My favorite, and most frequent, interview was with the legendary jazz pianist George Shearing. George and I spoke on a number of occasions in Columbus, two of which were followed by dinners at our home. I once traveled to Chicago to interview him for a half-hour documentary on behalf of the American Foundation for the Blind. I was even asked by *The Columbus Dispatch* to review a performance by his quintet at a local lounge.

On that occasion I had the opportunity to say in print what I've always felt about the man: *Where George Shearing is concerned, I'm a "groupie." And have been since before the word was coined. I couldn't be objective about this gentle and talented man if he were on trial for stoning a Steinway or bombing a Baldwin.*

George and I first met when I was employed by WRFD, and for reasons I can't recall, he came to the studio rather than my meeting him at his hotel. We had a fine interview, owing to his sheer exuberance for living and, despite being blind from childhood, a wonderfully playful sense of humor. As was by now my custom, at the end of the interview I invited him to dinner. George agreed, and in a rare display of advance planning, I asked him if there was anything he didn't eat. No, he was pretty much up for anything.

When he left the studio I phoned my bride to tell her that we were having a distinguished guest for dinner a few days hence. To her credit, Mary accepted the news calmly and even suggested we invite another couple and make a night of it. On the evening of the dinner, I picked George up at his hotel and drove him to our apartment. Waiting for us were Mary, a sorority sister of hers, and Jack Eby, whom you met in Chapter Two. Mary had produced the finest dinner our still meager income could afford: a lovely meat, cheese, sour cream, and pasta casserole; green salad; biscuits and jam; and for dessert homemade pumpkin pie. It pleased everyone in attendance. Except George, who ate nothing but the biscuits. He was gracious, assured Mary the meal was undoubtedly delicious, but that he simply didn't eat most of the dinner's ingredients. Mary shot me a withering glance, but for once I felt blameless. I'd done my part; my only mistake was believing what I had been told. When dinner was ended, we said goodnight to our guests and Mary and I drove George to the Maramor for his evening show, arriving early enough (at his request) for him to dine on liver and onions. There's no accounting for British tastes.

On another visit to our home, this time in a real house, George was introduced to our dear friends Marsha and Doug Kohler and Betsy and Fred Isaac. No slipups this time; Mary had settled on roast beef and Yorkshire pudding for the entrée. As we enjoyed drinks in our living room, George turned to Fred and said, "You're Jewish, aren't you?" Fred replied, "Yes," and ever the straight man, "How can you tell?" Eyes crinkled in anticipation George replied, "From the length of your voice."

OUT OF WORK and in need of a job to feed a growing
family, I was happy to become Columbus Taxi Driver No. 967.

In September 1960, as Mary's and my wedding day approached, I began to think of a way to celebrate the event with my coworkers at WRFD that would be memorable for them, as well as for me. Though I tried to think of alternatives, I kept coming back to an idea first mentioned to me by Bill Blinn, whom you also met in Chapter Two. Bill had once promised that on some occasion—graduation day, I think—he would show up with "a Thermos of mixed martinis." The phrase resonated with me, and I finally decided that was how I would begin my week's vacation that was to contain both a wedding and a brief honeymoon.

From this distance it seems a pretty benign breach of company policy, asking fellow staff members to join me in a toast in advance of my nuptials. But we are, after all, talking about WRFD. When I produced my Thermos and a handful of paper cups, it became an immediate test of corporate loyalty vs. company camaraderie. Some joined me, others stammered their apologies and slipped away. One saw fit to lecture me on the evils of drinking in general and the particular sin of doing so in the afternoon, somehow missing the point that by happy hour the station would be closed and locked. Station manager Joe Bradshaw quoted to me from the Nationwide Employees Policy Manual as he sipped from his cup with solemn eyes. It was yet another black mark in a growing list of transgressions that would inevitably be my undoing.

When I was finally summoned to Phil Sheridan's office following a Saturday afternoon shift, I was informed that I was being terminated with two weeks notice "for being a corrosive influence on the staff." It was a great line and absolutely accurate. As an employer myself for more than 30 years, I've thought many times that, given my work ethic and attitude at the time, I would have fired me, too. In the future Phil would rehire me at WRFD-FM and I would again leave, this time on my terms and after rehabilitating my reputation. It's a wonder what a little maturity will do. Once again, on the very day I am writing this, I've learned of Phil's passing. He was a good man.

Suddenly, if not unexpectedly unemployed, I needed a new job. Broadcasting was all I knew, but with Mary expecting the birth of our first child, I needed the interval between paychecks to be seamless. So while I made the rounds of Columbus radio and TV stations, I also explored "quick hire" opportunities. The first company to offer me a job was Northland Cab, if I secured the necessary permit and license. A visit to the Bureau of Motor Vehicles provided me with a copy of the rules and regulations I would need to know to pass the commercial driver's license exam, and after a few hours study I was able to do just that. A few days passed while I waited for the city to process my paperwork, and one morning the mail delivered the news that I was licensed as City of Columbus, Ohio Taxi Driver 967.

My career in urban transportation was mercifully brief, to the relief of all parties. I tended to use the two-way radio as I would if I were piloting an airliner, reporting my every move to the dispatcher. I was frequently told to shut up and get off the air. As noted earlier, I lacked both a native's familiarity with Columbus streets and a well developed sense of direction and so was frequently lost, necessitating more calls to the dispatcher. Finally, I could never remember to turn off the meter when I dropped off a fare. If the meter read ninety cents, I might be given a dollar and told to keep the change. I'd made a ten-cent tip ... until I pulled away from the curb with the meter still running and heard it click over to a dollar. At that point I owed the company the full dollar and my tip vanished. Years later someone asked me why I hadn't applied for unemployment compensation. The fact is it never occurred to me.

One of the benefits of driving a cab was that I frequently found myself in the vicinity of radio and TV stations. It was the perfect opportunity to run in and grab a minute or two of face time with the program manager or chief announcer and so demonstrate my continuing interest in a position with their company.

On one occasion I ran into WOSU-TV and tried to speak with station manager, David Ayers. He was out, but I was invited to fill in an employment application, which would be given to him on his return. I was told I could sit at his desk while I wrote.

As I finished with the application I noticed that Mr. Ayers had a daily calendar on his desk—the sort where each new day requires that you turn another page. Seized of an inspiration I turned the calendar ahead several days and wrote, "Hire Ken Keller." A few more days and I wrote "This would be a good day to hire Ken Keller." I made the same entry with varying words three or four times more, then left his office, turning in the application at the front desk. Sometime later, after I had been hired by WOSU Radio, I ran into David at a local saloon, The Blue Danube. Did he remember that I had once tried to work for him? Hell, yes, he did. He claimed that he kept running into my notes on his calendar for months after my visit. I don't think I made that many entries, but it's been a long time, and on this point, we may have to trust his memory.

Happily, my career as a taxi driver ended as abruptly as it began. I was offered and accepted a job with WOSU Radio, Ohio State's professionally staffed broadcast service and the first educational radio station in North America. The university received an experimental license to broadcast on April 20, 1920, and in 1922 was awarded the call letters WEAO which stood for, we are told, Willing, Energetic, Athletic Ohio. The WOSU call letters were granted the station in September 1933.

Never has such a glorious sound emanated from humbler facilities. Housed in a World War I-era electrical science laboratory that was little more than a brick shell of a building with warehouse-worthy concrete flooring, the depravations suffered by the staff as a consequence of such ill-housing were many and worth recalling.

To begin, there was no air-conditioning. Stultifying summer temperatures within the building were moderated only slightly by opening windows and one of the two doors that opened to the street. Fans were in use everywhere, but they only served to rearrange the already superheated air. Women members of the staff wore the sheerest of summer weight dresses and the men, already in short sleeve white shirts, had nowhere else to turn for relief. Engineers, who sat for long hours in close proximity to glowing vacuum tubes, were given the greatest latitude in terms of dress and sometimes came to work in bathing suits. Not infrequently during the day, airplanes on approach to, or departure from, Port Columbus, would pass in slow flight directly over the studios, their powerful piston engines creating such a din through the open windows that announcers or newscasters at work would simply stop reading until they could hear themselves again.

Winter brought another kind of hardship, for while there was a measure of heating in the building, it was steam heat passing through old and tired radiators that wheezed and clanged so badly that they had to be shut off during live broadcasts. An engineer whose name deserves, but has not received, a place in my memory once recorded a half hour or so of radiator sounds, then carefully ascribed a musical value to each clang and bonk. By cutting and splicing the tape according to his notes, he was able to produce a strange but not unlovely recording of several famous phrases from the classical music repertoire. Within the building's shell were many offices, all of whose walls unaccountably were constructed of the same material used in the making of bulletin boards. What the walls lacked in durability (chief announcer Gene Gerrard, enraged at an engineer who started a recording at the wrong speed, threw a glass ashtray at a studio wall that instantly stuck in its own hole) they made up for in practicality. Whenever you wished to keep a piece of paper in plain sight, you simply thumb-tacked it to the wall in front of you.

To provide a bit of comfort underfoot, as well as to deaden the sound of footsteps, old carpets had been scavenged from various places for use in the studios. Threadbare and thin, they nevertheless were home to a variety of insects and other creeping critters. Women who worked at WOSU had long-since lost any squeamishness about being in proximity to such coworkers and, when not otherwise employed, could dispatch a centipede with all the skill and deftness of a toreador.

The WOSU "sound" is most readily likened to today's National Public Radio, and not without reason. Several of the founding employees of NPR were former WOSU staffers. Classical music, news, and public affairs were the staples of the station, but there was so much more. A typical broadcast day also included French and German language courses; a cover-to-cover reading of some current best-seller served up in daily half-hour installments during *In the Bookstall* with Gene Gerrard; a sampling of world press editorial opinion gathered from newspapers in Germany, Sweden, France, Britain, Israel, and Japan; science programs such as *Doctor Tell Me* and *Men and Molecules*; and locally produced children's programs with names like *Once Upon a Time in Ohio, Boys and Girls in Bookland* and *Newspaper of the Air*. Writing for the children's audience was the responsibility of Margaret Tyler and Marion "Pat" Renick, the latter authoring more than thirty children's books in her lifetime. One of my first duties on arriving at WOSU was to play a horse in the broadcast version of a children's book.

Our afternoon "drive time" program, *On the Way Home*, was an hour-long magazine format show that bundled news, sports, market summaries, and weather forecasts together with movie and theatre reviews, jazz, recorded humor, and just about anything else that would bring a smile to someone stuck in five o'clock gridlock. It became the model for NPR's very successful *All Things Considered*, a story told to me by former WOSU station manager Don Quayle.

"When I was at Ohio State (1956-60), Al Hulsen, then the News Director, reformatted the 5 to 6 p.m. time slot by taking four fifteen minute programs and turning them into a one-hour magazine called *On the Way Home*, which was very successful.

"When I moved to WGBH in Boston (1960-62), I hired Al to work with me on a regional network of FM stations in the northeast called The Educational Radio Network. Having had success with a drive time program in Columbus, we started one on this network and called it *Kaleidoscope*. It was produced by Susan Stamberg, who was then on the staff of WAMU in Washington, DC. The ERN continued as an interconnected regional network until the Martin Luther King March on Washington in November of 1963. That was the last big event we covered live before the money for interconnection ran out.

"I was hired as the first president of NPR in August of 1970. I, in turn, hired Bill Siemering from WBFO in Buffalo. I told him that I wanted to begin with a ninety minute magazine program in drive time. After that, we would let the programming expand as staff and resources allowed. We had several discussions about magazine programming at drive time but the details of implementation were left up to Bill and the program staff. During the planning of the program, I took Bill to lunch with me one day to meet a person with whom I was acquainted and who had expressed an interest in working at NPR, even though it was new and she didn't know much about it. That person was Susan Stamberg. Susan was hired and came aboard to help design *All Things Considered* and, of course, hosted that program for many years."

I began work at WOSU as a staff announcer in June 1961. It was a shock and very soon a pleasure to be suddenly immersed in broadcasting classical music. There were hundreds of new and foreign names to learn to pronounce and a wealth of background and biographies of composers and performers to try to memorize. And the absolute and unchallenged authority for this schooling was our erudite, informed, and iconoclastic music director, Fred Calland.

Fred's principal task with the station, beyond his long-suffering attempts to impart a little basic knowledge to new announcers ("Ira is *not* George Gershwin's wife."), was to publish the music listings in the monthly program bulletin for listeners. No small task as doing so necessitated not only blending a wonderful variety of periods, instruments, and performers, but also making sure that every collection of recordings used in a given program aggregated in performance time no more than the duration of that program. Thus, because *Morning Show* was sixty minutes, the combined music selections for the show had to total about fifty-eight minutes, and because *Sunup Symphony* was thirty minutes, the music had to total about twenty-seven and a half minutes. Each weekday had six separate blocks of music. In addition to the two already mentioned, there were *Morning Melodies* (fifty-five minutes), *Afternoon Music* (ninety minutes), *Interlude* (thirty minutes) and *Evening Concert* (140 minutes). So, programming just one workweek of airtime involved thirty different blocks of music, to say nothing of the weekends.

To make matters worse, while record producers had begun putting the playing times of recordings on the labels of the records they sent to radio stations, these were frequently wrong, and not by just a little. So each new recording that came to the station had to be timed against a stopwatch and its running time noted on a three-by-five card that was added to one of several files above the music director's well-worn desk. Fred's job was more than full-time, frequently extending well into the evening and even late night hours, especially as the printing deadline for the program bulletin neared.

For all the pressure, Fred managed it with quiet dignity, though he never suffered fools gladly. One time a WOSU program director instructed Fred that he was to write a letter of apology to a listener who was offended by the fact that a piece of music published in the program bulletin did not air as promised. Reluctantly, Fred set about writing the letter. As he neared the end, he removed the actual letter from the typewriter but continued to type through the carbon paper to the second sheet (the one he would leave on the program director's desk): "In conclusion, I'm sorry that the selection you waited to hear did not air when promised but you must understand these little fuck-ups will occur." Fred was at breakfast and well out of earshot when the program director read his copy of the letter.

Don Quayle also remembers Fred. "He was the one person I knew about whom I could actually say, 'He was a genius.' I was known to be hard to break up when on-air, but Fred accomplished it one day when he came into the small studio near the record library and did a complete strip in front of me until he was buck naked. I used the 'cough button' (to close a live mic) more than I ever had before.

"Later, I hired Fred at NPR and Al (Hulsen) hired Diana (Fred's wife) at CPB (Corporation for Public Broadcasting). I do believe they still have a quilt of Fred's hanging in the lobby at NPR. But don't get me started on Fred stories ... there are too many of them."

In July of 1962, I was promoted to news supervisor of the WOSU radio stations, working under news director Don Davis. It was while working in the news department that I became reacquainted with Charlie Pickard, acquiring in the process another lifelong friend.

Charlie and his mother had been frequent visitors to WRFD, arriving, as I had with my mother, to watch radio being "made." It was a pleasure to spend time with this bright, eager, and unfailingly polite young man and to answer his questions about radio. And then one day, there he was in the newsroom—a student at Ohio State and the newest member of the WOSU staff.

Charlie had been recruited into radio by a poster he'd seen on campus soliciting volunteer actors for *Ohio School of the Air*. Ed Talbert was in charge of *OSA* production and Charlie was soon appearing on *Boys and Girls in Bookland* and *Once Upon a Time in Ohio*. Pleased with his eager new volunteer, Ed asked Charlie if he'd like to become a part-time employee, recording and editing speeches given at the university for later broadcast on WOSU. Charlie quickly agreed, and a future civil engineer began to recede into the mists. In the fall of 1962, Charlie became a full-time staff announcer and later sports director. In this latter role he was soon a regular in the newsroom.

Charlie had a natural inquisitiveness—a necessary and highly desirable quality for a fledgling newsman. But he also had a tendency to want to have every question answered for him before beginning an assignment. One day I sat him down across from me and asked if he had ever heard the story of the message to Garcia. He hadn't, so I explained. Or rather, I let Elbert Hubbard explain. "When war broke out between Spain and the United States, it was very necessary to communicate quickly with the leader of the Insurgents. Garcia was somewhere in the mountain vastness of Cuba—no one knew where. No mail nor telegraph message could reach him. The President must secure his cooperation, and quickly."

"What to do?"

The solution, as it turned out, was to entrust the message to Major Andrew Summers Rowan, an 1881 West Point graduate, who famously accepted the assignment to locate Garcia without asking where he was or how to find him. Four days later, Rowan landed by night off the coast of Cuba, disappeared into the jungle, and three weeks later came out on the other side of the island having delivered the letter.

"By the Eternal! There is a man whose form should be cast in deathless bronze and the statue placed in every college of the land. It is not book-learning young men need, nor instruction about this and that, but a stiffening of the vertebrae which will cause them to be loyal to a trust, to act promptly, concentrate their energies, do the thing: 'Carry a message to Garcia!'"

Charlie listened intently to my words and seemed to understand. I knew I had made my point when, the next morning, I found on my desk Charlie's parody of the lyrics to "Maria" from *West Side Story:*

Garcia.

Has anyone here seen Garcia?

He's sort of round and fat

I don't know where he's at

Do you?

Garcia.

I've got a note here for Garcia.

It's from the president

He said when it was sent, "Get through."

Garcia.

Say it loud and can't get near it.

Say it soft and you almost can't hear it.

Garcia. Has anyone here seen Garcia?

Several additional verses followed, one having to do with "bullets and beer," but as my memory is imprecise, and I have no desire to approximate Charlie's wit, I'll leave the lyrics incomplete.

Chapter seven

At a point when the local television stations were chest-thumping about various awards that their newscasts had won, I remarked facetiously to Charlie that what our newscasts required was an award that would level the playing field. A few days later I was delighted to receive a letter and small engraved plaque proclaiming me the first (and only) winner of the Charles M. Pickard Award for Distinguished Newscasting. The plaque, somewhat the worse for its age and frequent moves, still hangs in my office.

Charlie was drafted into the Army in December 1963, and spent most of the next two years in Panama. Upon returning to civilian life, Charlie immediately sought his fortune in commercial radio, eventually working for, and being fired by, the difficult-to-please Phil Sheridan. After this, Charlie became one of the most successful freelance voice talents in the area and was, for many years, the statewide voice of Big Bear stores. As with Bill Hamilton, I was pleased to hire Charlie on a number of occasions to record commercials and industrial videos for my advertising agency. As I write, Charlie continues his freelance career and also works the occasional shift at our shared alma mater, WOSU Radio.

PRESS BOX PASS for the Ohio State vs. Michigan game of 1961. Ohio State won handily, 50 to 20.

In September of 1964, I was appointed program director of WOSU AM and FM and so began my first desk job in broadcasting. Short of renewing program contracts and trying to understand how the university budget worked, there was little to keep me occupied. But as I noted earlier, radio was in a state of transition as it sought to retain an audience that more and more was falling under the thrall of network television. In a bid to attract more youthful listeners, WBNS Radio, the local CBS affiliate, decided to drop its weekly broadcasts of the New York Philharmonic. Adding them to the WOSU program lineup was a natural. When I explored the possibility of doing so, I was given a green light by the station manager with the unnecessary admonition that there was no money in the budget to pay for them.

Adjacent to the Ohio State campus was, and is, the sprawling complex of Battelle Memorial Institute. A partner with OSU in many research projects, I wondered if it might partner with us in presenting the Philharmonic broadcasts. Following a number of telephone calls, I managed to catch the attention of Battelle's public affairs office and, eventually, its director, Bob Stith. Bob was a fan both of the Philharmonic broadcasts and the WOSU stations, and in due course, Battelle agreed to pick up the tab for the full 1964-65 broadcast season. I worked with Bob in preparing a series of what today would be called "infomercials," explaining some of the research then in progress at Battelle, and we recorded these to run during the sixty-second commercial breaks in the broadcasts.

It may not have been the first time off-campus money was used to underwrite station programming, but I'm not aware of any similar undertaking that predates it.

Don Leshner, the WOSU announcer I was hired to replace, had an interesting feature of his job description. He had been the colorcaster for Ohio State football broadcasts on WOSU, and as his replacement, it was simply assumed that I would take on this role, together with Don's announcing shifts. It was a dismaying prospect. Even then, Ohio State was a tradition-rich football powerhouse, and everyone connected with the program was assumed to be the best in their craft. Our play-by-play announcer, Marv Homan, didn't disappoint.

Before big money contracts limited the radio coverage to a single station, there were frequently as many as four Columbus stations originating broadcasts of every game, along with other stations from major cities around Ohio. Then, too, there were usually several stations from the opposing team's city and state. Of all the play-by-play announcers from all those stations, I never heard one as good as Marv. His full-time job as Ohio State's Assistant Sports Information Director responsible for, among other things, assembling each year's media guides to Ohio State sports, gave him top-of-mind access to a wealth of background data on each team member and coach. And his natural Midwestern reserve and courtesy made him a welcome guest in every home. The four years Marv and I spent working Ohio State football games, home and away, remain among my happiest radio memories.

WOSU's coverage of Ohio State football was deemed to be the official broadcast, and so Marv and I traveled as members of the official family.

We flew with the team, dined with them, and shared the same hotel as well. The reader would be forgiven for thinking this brought me into close contact with team members, but this was not the case. There was a distance between players and coaches on the one hand and the official family on the other. It was a distance I never saw anyone try to bridge, even when sitting across an airplane aisle from a budding All-American. The reason for this, as for everything else having to do with OSU football, was head coach Wayne Woodrow "Woody" Hayes.

Coach Hayes was not merely the absolute master of his team in practice and on the field; he was the final authority on the conduct of team members in most aspects of their private lives as well. WBNS-TV's post-game shows with the coach provided a peek into these relationships. Paul Hornung, sports editor of *The Columbus Dispatch*, was the interviewer; the day's standout player was the interviewee; and Coach Hayes the ever-present interlocutor.

Paul: *Bill* (to pick a name), *it looked like you were having trouble picking up the blitz in the first half of today's game.*

Coach Hayes: *Well, now, that's right, he didn't see the coverage, did ya, Bill?*

Bill: *That's right, Coach.*

Coach Hayes: *No sir, didn't see it coming. Not a bit. But we got that sorted out at halftime, didn't we, Bill?*

Bill: *That's right, Coach.*

Coach Hayes: *Brought our ends in tight and got the fullback to start picking up the first man through. Bought us another second or two to spot the open man. Really helped your throwing, didn't it, Bill?*

Bill: *That's right, Coach.*

Coach Hayes: *You're darn right.*

A fictitious exchange, to be sure, but a fair approximation of the way Coach Hayes permitted "interviews" with his team.

To demonstrate the extent of the fiction in the above interview, consider that the exchange implies that Ohio State actually threw the football. Under Coach Hayes it almost never did. I once interviewed the coach in the locker room inside cavernous Ohio Stadium when he famously, though probably not for the first time, said "I still believe it's more important to put air in the football than to put the football in the air."

One of my most vivid memories of Coach Hayes in action occurred in 1964 when Ohio State flew to Iowa City to take on the Iowa Hawkeyes. As Iowa City was too small to support a major airport, the team actually flew to Cedar Rapids and then took buses into the college town. Following Coach Hayes' game plan for the entire weekend, the buses stopped first at Kinnick Stadium where the team went through a light workout, testing the footing of the field they would be playing on the next day. Then it was back aboard the buses and on to the hotel for room assignments, unpacking, and lunch. Following lunch, the team usually went to a movie together, but this day would be different.

Just ten days before, former President Herbert Hoover had passed away in New York City at the age of ninety, and just three days earlier had been buried on the grounds of the Herbert Hoover Presidential Library in West Branch, Iowa—a short drive east on I-80 from Iowa City.

Ever the history professor that his credentials included, Coach Hayes loaded his charges back aboard the buses for a visit to the library. After a stop at the gravesite, the team trooped into the library's small auditorium where they were met by a diminutive, white-haired man who began, probably for the hundredth time that week, to tell the story of America's 31st president.

Coach Hayes listened quietly for several minutes, then jumped to his feet and, using his considerable bulk to gently edge the smaller man out of the way, began his own lecture on President Hoover's legacy by saying, "Yes, yes, Hoover was a good president but he wasn't a *great* one. And the reason is, he never played football."

For a moment I couldn't believe what I'd heard. Was some part of my brain finishing sentences for maximum comic effect? Two things convinced me I had heard correctly. For one, the small man who had begun the lecture was now frozen in open-mouthed, uncomprehending wonder at what was happening right in front of him. For another, my companions at the back of the auditorium, *Columbus Citizen-Journal* sportswriter Kaye Kessler and Marv, had both suddenly found something intensely interesting on the floor and were bent over in their seats, their shoulders heaving in silent synchronization.

Coach Hayes went on to deliver an interesting, some might say startling, appraisal of the Great Depression and how it could have been shortened if President Hoover had simply employed the rules of teamwork and discipline that are well understood by even the least accomplished football player.

Another football weekend that will live in my memory is the game that wasn't played. It was the fourth Friday in November 1963, and Marv and I were in Ypsilanti, Michigan, where the team was staying the day before its date with the University of Michigan Wolverines. It was early afternoon; lunch was ended, and we had returned to our hotel room to let the traditional steak-and-baked-potato training table meal digest. As we sat in silence, I reached for the portable radio that I always carried on the road. The skies were dull and gray, and I hoped I could catch a weather report that would tell us if snow was in the forecast.

I tuned to a local CBS affiliate. It was a few minutes past 1:30 p.m. and the network was running the radio version of a newspaper staple, *Dear Abby*. As we listened, the audio feed suddenly stopped. There was a long period of silence, then the sound of confusion. I thought I could make out the clacking of newsroom teletype machines behind the babble of voices just off microphone. Then a newsman—Alan Jackson, I believe—told us that shots had been fired at President Kennedy's motorcade in Dallas and that the presidential limousine was seen leaving the motorcade. Thus began our nation's long and draining collective nightmare.

I don't recall what activity was planned to occupy the team that afternoon, but it was cancelled without a word being spoken. As each new and horrible detail was reported on radio and TV, the hotel became quieter, no one venturing away from whatever news source had first caught their attention. When the president was pronounced dead, it was as if all the air left our room. Much later I found myself on the first floor of our hotel and, turning a corner, ran into Coach Hayes. I mentioned to him that, given the events of the day, it might be appropriate to invite a clergyperson to join us for the evening meal. The Coach looked through me as he did anyone who didn't carry a football, mumbled a few words, and continued on his way, but that evening there was a Catholic priest in our midst who had been summoned to provide a few words of comfort. Astonishingly, his invocation was entirely about the game of football and contained not a single reference to the tragedy in Dallas.

As the evening wore on, news reporting began to center on reaction across the United States and around the world. First one and then dozens of football games that were to be played the following day were cancelled. Ohio State-Michigan was not one of them. Epic in its storied rivalry, it was still difficult to believe that "The Game" would be played against a backdrop of national mourning, but that was our understanding when we went to bed that night.

Sometime early Saturday morning, three large buses filled with Ohio State's marching band, their instruments, instrument cases, and uniforms left Columbus headed for Ann Arbor. About 10 a.m. word was finally circulated that our game, too, had been cancelled, or more accurately, postponed for a week. An intern in the WOSU newsroom and a member of the marching band told us later how band director Jack Evans didn't get word of the postponement until he stepped off the bus in Ann Arbor. The director was seething as the buses turned around and began the three-hour trip back to Columbus. Racing into his office in the band room, Evans slammed the door behind him but could still be heard shouting into a telephone, "Do you mean to tell me that the highway patrols of two states couldn't find three Greyhounds traveling bumper-to-bumper and stop them before we made the whole trip?"

My first year as Marv's colorman was a carbon copy of Don Leshner's last year in this role as I sought out Marv's advice on what to do and when to do it. Home games typically began at 1:15 p.m. We would take the air at 1 p.m., providing fifteen minutes of welcome, including a description of the weather, stadium, crowd, pre-game band show, facts about Big Ten and national rankings, and an introduction of the players. These fifteen minutes were mine to fill, and Marv was frequently not in the booth. As the teams came out on the field for kickoff, I handed the broadcast over to Marv and assumed my second role as a member of the broadcast team.

Marv had cleverly made little wooden trays with slots representing every position of a football team lined up in T-formation. There was one tray for the Buckeyes and one for the opponent.

On one side of each tray were slots for the offense and on the reverse were slots for the defense. Beneath spring-loaded clamps were slips of index-weight paper with the jersey number, name, height, weight, hometown, and college major of each person apt to play that position during a game. Once the game was underway, I was to indicate with a point of my finger who was the ball carrier or, less likely, receiver on offense or who had made the tackle on defense. If the Buckeyes were defending the goal to our left, I sat on Marv's left. To his right was another spotter doing the exact same thing for the opposing team. At the end of the quarter, the other spotter and I would exchange seats. The result was that Marv had a ready reference of who was in the game playing what position, lined up exactly as the teams were on the field below us.

When the first timeout arrived, I assumed my third role on the team. As the originating station for a network of some fifteen commercial radio stations around Ohio, it was necessary to provide sixty-second commercial cutaways throughout the broadcast. But WOSU was a non-commercial public radio station so we had to fill the same sixty seconds with public service announcements. Once Marv gave the cutaway cue, "This is the Ohio State Football Network," my job—stopwatch in hand—was to provide exactly sixty seconds worth of PSAs, then link the network back up with a few words of transition and hand the mic back to Marv.

How this process worked with our network stations is perhaps worth the telling. Amazing as it seems today, given the enormous sums of money that change hands over major college athletics, as recently as the early 1960s most schools were more favored by the publicity their athletic broadcasts generated than by the revenue. I still have copies of the contracts I executed in 1964 as WOSU Program Director with fifteen Ohio radio stations. A full season's revenue from broadcast rights for seven games provided to all fifteen stations amounted to $4,602.50. Rights fees ranged from a high of $150 per game (WHIO Dayton) to a low of $29.25 (WCSM Celina and WPTW Piqua). Rates were determined by the "published daytime, one-time, national rate applicable to the station;" in other words, what that station would charge a national client for one sixty-second spot to air during its daytime hours.

Given the low commercial fees charged by these stations, they were not in a position to pay more for the broadcast rights. They were also not eager to incur the cost of a telephone line from Columbus to get the broadcast signal to their stations. As a consequence, all the stations on our network used what is called air-to-air relay. They would literally receive the WOSU signal on a tuner in their studios and rebroadcast it, until they heard a cutaway cue. Then they would override our signal with their own commercial delivered from their own studio. After sixty seconds we'd all get together again in the press box. But what if a station was located so far from Columbus that it couldn't receive the WOSU signal? The solution for that station was to rebroadcast the signal of some other station that was located closer to Columbus and *was* receiving and transmitting the WOSU signal. In this "bucket brigade" fashion, our football broadcasts were passed around the state.

When halftime arrived Marv would leave the booth for a few minutes of well deserved rest, and I would settle in to describe the colorful band shows that were a favorite of our listeners. With fewer commercial commitments than the other local originators, and with our built-in need to promote the whole of the university, WOSU made a specialty of covering all the music and pageantry of Big Ten halftime shows. The Ohio State University Marching Band, "The Best Damn Band in the Land," passed out diagrams and descriptions of its halftime formations to the media to assist in their coverage of its performance. Still, I believe we were the only station to confine our commentary to the lulls between musical numbers and to do our best to pick up the all-brass sound of the band using a roof-mounted microphone and parabolic reflector. We, of course, extended the same courtesy to the visiting band. If you are an Ohio State graduate, the band is only a tick lower in your affections than the team, and we regularly received thank-you notes from listeners around the state for our halftime coverage.

From the standpoint of our broadcasts, the third and fourth quarters were identical to the first two. When the game ended, a frantic press box aide would dash into our broadcast booth with a mimeographed sheet of game statistics. Marv would summarize the game, making use of the stats thus provided, then turn the mic back to me for a final description of the scene in front of us and to set the scene for next week's game. The wrap-up included thanking one or two of our network stations, and then we threw the broadcast back to our studios. In that instant, the network collapsed as each station went back to its own programming.

As I moved into my second, and subsequent, years of working with Marv, I began to suggest changes to our working relationship,

most of which Marv generously supported. For one thing, I
suggested that WOSU, not the Athletic Department, assume
responsibility for pitching the network to Ohio radio stations in
advance of the season, determining the fees to be charged and
issuing contracts for broadcast rights. Marv quickly agreed and this
became our new practice. For another, in order to provide some
vocal variety during the broadcasts, I got our engineering staff to
carry a portable tape deck into the press box for home games. This
allowed us to intersperse pre-recorded player interviews and public
service announcements throughout the broadcast so that Marv and
I were not the only voices heard for three and a half hours.

Visiting stadiums around the country was a delight, and I
looked forward to the courtesies that were unfailingly extended to
us by the host schools' athletic departments. All except one. The
University of Minnesota conceded nothing to other schools in its
hospitality, but the radio level of its stadium press box scared the
hell out of me. The back walls of the broadcast booths were flush
with the outside wall of the stadium. To enter them, you had to
inch your way along an open catwalk that was suspended maybe
fifty feet in the air above the concrete sidewalk that ringed the
outside of the stadium. I have more than a touch of acrophobia,
and that walk into and out of the Golden Gophers' press box was
the truest test of my company loyalty. Actually, walk is too strong
a word. It was more like a creep, with my back pressed tightly
against the wooden slats that were the outside back walls of the
booths. I was careful not to drink anything from breakfast onward
that would necessitate a trip out of the booth during the broadcast.

One Friday, Marv and I joined the team for a flight from
Columbus to Los Angeles and a date the following day with the

UCLA Bruins in venerable Memorial Coliseum. We deplaned at Los Angeles International Airport and boarded busses for our hotel. We did, but our luggage didn't, though we were not to know that for several hours. Our plane, my clean tidy-whities, Marv's miraculous spotter trays, and all my broadcast formats and public service announcements stayed aboard the plane and were soon on their way to Honolulu.

It was unusual, but not unprecedented, for our luggage not to be in our hotel room when we came back from lunch. But as the afternoon dragged on we became nervous enough to seek out the United Airlines representative who always traveled in our party. More time was lost as he made the required calls and learned that we were, indeed, luggage-less. Owing to the time change, it was now too late to do any good back in Columbus, so we began to map our plans for game day.

The time change would work in our favor the next morning; by the time we awoke at 6 a.m. there would be someone who could help me at the station. What I needed was for them to locate my duplicate copies of all the scripts and formats I had brought with me and read them to me over the phone as I transcribed them longhand. It would be a tedious business but it beat ad-libbing through ten or twelve commercial cutaways.

The real problem was replacing Marv's spotter trays. Without these Marv was looking at filling 210 minutes of airtime with nothing but descriptions of the action in front of him, sometimes without being sure who the players on the field were, to say nothing of lacking access to the wealth of background data that these trays also provided. We put our heads together, but no solution came to mind. The next morning after breakfast I was on my way back to the room to begin transcribing scripts and formats over the telephone when I spotted a florist shop off the hotel lobby. A thought came to mind, and I sought out the clerk to beg her for a couple dozen corsage pins, a corsage box, and a few lengths of tape. Back in the hotel room I located a program for the day's game and tore out the pages with the lineups for the two teams. Then I cut the corsage box into pieces, keeping the two long side panels and throwing everything else away. Finally, I taped one lineup to each box panel. Now I could stick a corsage pin through the lineup adjacent to the name of any player in the game and cause it to stick in the cardboard beneath. And to the right of the name was most of the players' data that Marv's spotter trays contained.

When I showed the arrangement to Marv he agreed that it was better than nothing, with some notable drawbacks. For one, every time offense became defense, every pin would have to be pulled and reset into new names. And because of this, probably well before the end of the game, the cardboard would become so riddled with pinholes that it might not continue to hold pins upright.

I spent the next couple of hours transcribing the formats and scripts I would need, then boarded one of several team buses for the trip to Memorial Coliseum. Marv and I carried our makeshift gear up to the press box and began to settle in for the broadcast. The football field at Memorial Coliseum was then a breathtaking distance below the press box and separated even further by the width of an Olympic-size track that encircled the field. When UCLA took the field for its pre-game warm-up, we were horrified to see that they were wearing powder blue jerseys with white numerals. The separating distance, a bright Los Angeles sun, and poor color contrast between jerseys and numerals made it almost impossible to identify their players. When things go bad, they go very bad, indeed.

As airtime approached, we made a vow to give it our best efforts. Three, two, one, and the broadcast began. We were not only feeding WOSU listeners and our network, but also the Armed Forces Radio Network as well. Our least prepared-for broadcast was enjoying its largest audience of the year. I had been on the air for about ten minutes when I heard a commotion behind me: voices (unusual in a press box during a broadcast) and much thumping and bumping. I closed it out of my mind and continued to talk. Suddenly, there was Marv beside me, grinning broadly and holding his spotter trays. A moment later and my three-ring binder filled with formats and scripts was placed in front of me. They had enjoyed a very brief visit to the islands before being placed on an eastbound flight back to the mainland and then special delivered directly to the press box. Once everything was unpacked, the remainder of the day went smoothly, though not for the Buckeyes. They lost to the Bruins 7-9. To this day I wonder if we could have successfully completed the broadcast with our corsage pin contraption.

now entering the game

THE WHITE PIANO
Chapter nine

OHIO GOVERNOR John J. Gilligan welcomes statehouse visitors to the Columbus Symphony's Brown Bag Concert, which I am about to narrate.

Whatever rewards of the spirit working for WOSU might have afforded, a decent wage was not part of the package. My Notice of Appointment as Radio TV Announcer I, dated June 8, 1961, shows an annual salary of $3,780, or approximately $23,600 in present value. For reference, the poverty level for a family of four, also expressed in today's dollars, is $19,157. In our first years as husband and wife, giving gifts was not in our budget. For our second Christmas together, I presented Mary with a much-needed garbage can (with matching lid). To mark the occasion of her graduation from Ohio State, I took advantage of an American Red Cross promotion and exchanged a pint of blood for a dozen red roses.

The practical consequence of the university's tight salary policy was that almost everyone who worked for WOSU held a second job. For many of us on the air-staff, that second employer was WBNS Radio. WBNS signed on in 1924 and by the early 1960s was the city's premier radio service. Affiliated with the CBS Network, WBNS's call letters reminded listeners that the owner's holdings included a **B**ank (Ohio National), a **N**ewspaper (*The Columbus Dispatch*), and a **S**hoe manufacturer (Wear-U-Well Shoes). My memory is that at least four of WOSU's fulltime air staff held part-time jobs at WBNS.

Mornings on WBNS were presided over by an avuncular professor from Ohio State named Irwin Johnson but known to generations of central Ohio listeners as "The Early Worm."

Late mornings were tended by Les Spencer, and the afternoon host was Dean Lewis. The all-night show was left in the hands of Bill Corley; newscasts were assembled and reported by Don Smith,

Chet Long and Ted Shell; sports by Marty DeVictor. Evenings and weekends were watched over by an assortment of part-timers, including my friends from WOSU.

Once I was clued in to how university salaries were supplemented, I quickly asked for and received a job interview with WBNS. My audition was conducted by chief announcer Russ Canter, one of the "Toledo voices" I remembered growing up with. In addition to working fulltime for WBNS, Russ had a contract with the Ohio Fuel Gas Company to serve as co-host of a daily tape recorded radio program called *The Betty Newton Show* that was syndicated to stations around the state, including one in Toledo. "Betty Newton girls" were hired by the gas company to visit the homes of customers who had just had new gas ranges installed to make sure they were familiar with all the features of their new appliances. The radio program helped to fashion the fiction of Betty Newton as a woman well-versed in the homely arts, and Russ served as the kindly, but clueless, male foil of the program's hostess.

So familiar had the name Russ Canter become in my growing-up home that once, when my parents were visiting Mary and me in Columbus and Russ called to discuss a change in my work assignment, my mother—hearing me refer to the caller as Russ—strode up to the phone and demanded to talk with this man whom she had never met. A startled, but accommodating, Russ spent several minutes on the phone chatting with my mother as befitted two friends of many years standing.

My audition was conducted in a large studio just off the WBNS lobby, then located on a floor near the top of the First National Building at 33 North High Street. Amusingly, I later learned that my great uncle Nicholas Schlee was president of the New First

National Bank when it moved into its new home on the ground floor of this very building. There didn't seem to be any way of *not* following about in great uncle Nick's shoes. Once I was settled behind a microphone in this studio that once housed the WBNS staff orchestra, Russ's disembodied voice floated over a speaker from the control room and told me to begin reading the sheets of news and commercials that I had been handed. After several minutes, he stopped me in mid-read and said, "OK, now describe the piano in front of you."

The ad lib test. Could I fill a couple of minutes of airtime with essentially nothing and still make it sound like something. My eyes sought out the piano, and I was relieved to see that it was painted a gleaming white. Well, that's a place to start, anyway. OK, here goes. "Well, you're not going to believe what I'm seeing folks, certainly not those of you who grew up, as I did, with a baby grand piano tucked into the corner of your living room. I mean, who can't remember the sight of that richly polished dark wood cabinet sitting atop three stalwart legs looking, for all the world, like a fort on stilts." (Not bad for openers. I wonder how long this is supposed to go on?) "Well, the piano in front of me is anything but 'richly polished dark wood.' In fact, it doesn't appear to be wood at all. And the reason is—it's white. Yes, that's right; the piano in front of me is pure white." (Jeez, that's it. I got nothing more. But he hasn't stopped me, so say something.) "Now, the question is, uh, does a white piano sound any different, uh, from a dark wood piano. And the answer would have to be—uh, I don't really know. I mean, you could suppose it might, uh, but I'd really have to hear, uh, the two of them, side by side, to, uh, really know. And, uh, even then— " Mercifully, I heard the soft click of the intercom indicating the ad lib test was over. I'm almost sure I also heard a soft, sadistic chuckle.

Despite my struggle to make the white piano fascinating to listeners, Russ hired me, and I was soon part of the cadre of part-timers that maintained the WBNS sound when the first-string talent was at their rest. I mostly worked weekends, with a liberal sprinkling of mid- and late-evening hours for good measure. The happy fact that WBNS needed so many part-time announcers can be traced to a sea of change in broadcasting that was just then starting to gain momentum. FM radio had been developed during World War II as a way of getting entertainment to the frontline troops and propaganda to the people of occupied Europe. As FM frequencies became available in postwar America, established AM stations made sure they each owned one without any clear idea of what they were going to do with it. In the short run, they simply simulcast their AM signal on their FM channel. But the Federal Communications Commission soon began letting AM station owners know that this wasn't what it had in mind when it granted them FM frequencies, and that it wanted more and more of the broadcast day to be programmed separately on the two services.

Many stations complied by purchasing great reels of "elevator music," which they played incessantly on their FM channels. Controlled by a bank of timers or by strips of foil placed at intervals on the music tape to trigger sensors, these reels would play for about fourteen minutes, stop at the end of a song (or sometimes in the middle of one), cause a recorded commercial or two to play (at a fraction of the cost to advertisers of an AM commercial), then restart the music for another fourteen minutes. The system needed minimal supervision and only broke down a couple of times each day.

But about the time I began working for WBNS, some station owners around the country were discovering that there *was* an audience for FM's unique clarity of sound if the station could find the right music for its market. WBNS was up for the challenge and began to wean itself from elevator music through the weekday mid- and late-evening hours. Uncertain as to what the "right" music might be for 7 p.m. to midnight, it programmed two hours of adult contemporary, followed by two hours of classical, and ending with one hour of jazz.

To tie this mix of formats together, WBNS hired a young announcer who had also begun his career in commercial radio at WMNI. Frederick Peerenboom, "the only Dutch-Sicilian in radio," brought an extraordinarily mellow voice, a love for all music, and a passion for jazz to the microphone, and listeners responded, forcing the station to let him identify himself on-air in place of the anonymity the station had previously insisted upon. In later years, Frederick was shortened to Fritz, Mr. Peerenboom moved from WBNS Radio to WBNS-TV, and the late night movie host "Fritz, the Night Owl" was born. At this writing, Fritz is doing a weekly jazz show on a pair of Smooth Jazz stations, his forty-eighth year of uninterrupted broadcasting in Columbus.

One interesting experiment that had nothing to do with folk music was an early attempt to deliver stereo music to the home by radio. For a couple of hours each evening, WBNS would play stereo recordings, sending one channel of music over its AM service and the other channel simultaneously over FM. The listener at home was instructed to sit facing both receivers, with AM on the left and FM on the right. If you managed to adjust the volumes just right and picked the perfect place to sit, you could (sometimes) hear a bit of stereo. Problem was there were almost no stereo recordings for the station to play. The big name of the moment in stereo was Enoch Light and the Light Brigade, whose every recording famously featured tunable tom-toms that swung back and forth between speakers to leave no room for doubt that THIS WAS STEREO! But when you were forced to listen to the same music night after night, the appeal faded and the experiment came to an end.

A major advantage to the owner of an FM station was the opportunity to commit small-audience programming to the FM frequency—programming that generated some revenue but was otherwise an audience killer. For WBNS, this was Cleveland Indians baseball. Move it from AM to FM and you could continue to realize some income from advertising, secure in the knowledge that diehard fans would find a way to listen, while at the same time reserving your AM frequency for the mainstream audience (it wasn't until the mid-1970s that the FM audience surpassed AM). In an unintended act of savagery, Russ Canter assigned me to ride the board through weekend Indians' baseball games.

Now, in addition to being forced to listen to a game I didn't admire, chained to a tiny studio for no other purpose than to read or play a commercial or two between half-innings, I discovered what happens when a building's air conditioning system can't differentiate between one studio large enough to house an orchestra and another small enough to be rejected as a telephone booth. The larger studio remains comfortable throughout July and August; the smaller one becomes a frozen food locker. Dressed in sweaters and gloves, my nose not responding to touch, I had endless hours to ponder, and even build on, my lifetime aversion to the great American pastime.

By way of making amends for Indians baseball, Russ also assigned me to work a late night program called *Music 'til One*. Sponsored by George Byers' Sons Chrysler Plymouth, the 105-minute nightly music program followed Ted Shell News at 11:15 p.m. and had a number of hosts during the course of a week. Play a few records, read one of several commercials provided by Byers' ad agency, play a few more records and repeat to fill an hour and forty-five minutes of the night. It was a job for my fellow part-timers; it was heaven for me—my favorite audience at my favorite time of the day.

Inspired by the station's move to real multiplex stereo broadcasting and plagued by the aforementioned lack of stereo recordings in the WBNS music library, I made friends with the owner of a record store on North High Street. Al Franz owned Discount Records, and he was as eager to build a customer base for his store as I was to build an audience for my program. We casually discussed "an arrangement" by which, in exchange for a mention or two of his store during the broadcasts, Al would let me have a copy of every new stereo recording that he received. The arrangement had to be casual; if it violated FCC rules, it certainly was not something that WBNS would sanction. But Enoch Light and the Light Brigade could only take you so far. Thanks to Al, I had access to the best, and most current, stereo library of any station in town. One problem solved; one problem remained.

The commercials I was given to read were not well done. They were poorly written, predictable, and sometimes even ungrammatical. A few nights into hosting this program, I laid the commercials aside and just began talking to the audience about my experience with Byers. The preceding winter, without any thought that I would one day be their spokesperson, Mary and I bought a new Plymouth Valiant from Byers. Still poor as church mice, the car we bought was stripped down about as much as a car could be: six cylinders, straight stick, rubber floor mats, and a radio as the only "option at additional cost." Despite this, the people at Byers had treated us as if we were buying the most expensive Chrysler in the showroom. And this is what I talked about. This, and what an incredibly serviceable car our Valiant was proving to be. The log called for twenty-one sixty-second commercials during the 105 minutes of the broadcast, or one every five minutes. I reduced the number of commercials by half and made them only as long as they needed to be to make a sales point. Now I had a program I could be proud of, at least on those nights when I was assigned as host.

One day at WOSU the phone rang in the newsroom. It was Dorrit Davis with Byers' ad agency. Would I consider hosting *Music 'til One* on a permanent basis? The client had heard what I was doing with the program, liked it, and wanted me to do it every night. This, I later learned, was not entirely true; George Byers, Sr. was an old man and went to bed well before the program began. But he had a long-time customer who did stay up that late at night, and she had convinced him he should hire me to do the show. Mrs. Ray O'Donnell was a name I had come to identify with lovely and gracious letters written longhand in green ink on blue stationery and occasional tins of homemade mincemeat cookies that would be waiting for me at the reception desk. It was she who had mentioned to her longtime friend that I was worth adding to the Byers' stable of talent that also included *Bill Pepper News* on WBNS-TV and Gene Fullen's *Byers' Bandwagon* on WTVN Radio.

I would be paid a talent fee of ten dollars per broadcast, in addition to the hourly wages WBNS paid all part-timers who worked the show. I didn't even ask for time to think about it.

Mrs. O'Donnell had performed a great service for me, and I am everlastingly in her debt. She also hosted one of the most uncomfortable evenings I have ever spent. A widow, Mrs. O'Donnell decided that she wanted Mary and me to meet her children and their spouses, and so arranged a dinner party at her home. When we arrived, the "children" proved to be considerably older, wealthier, and more established than we, and uncertain what to make of mother's strange new hobby of befriending broadcasters. We chatted long enough to establish that we had nothing in common, not even a shared history of Columbus, and the conversation began to falter. Hoping to inject some humor into the evening, Mrs. O'Donnell cautioned her children to "Be careful, I just may want to change my will." For the O'Donnell children and their spouses, this was an acknowledgement of the hippopotamus in the kitchen, and following a little strained laughter, a phalanx of four quietly arranged itself around Mrs. O'Donnell like destroyers around an aircraft carrier. The evening air turned decidedly frosty.

It seemed to take the better part of a week for us to admire Mrs. O'Donnell's African violets, dinner to be served, goodbyes to be spoken, and for us to escape to the dark and waiting Valiant. I remember receiving only a couple more letters with green ink on blue stationery (my father was the only other person I knew who routinely wrote in green ink), and then I completely lost track of Mrs. O' Donnell. I can't imagine it was by her choice; I know it wasn't by mine.

George Byers, Sr. was charmed by the idea of my non-commercials for his dealership and suggested that I drive a different new car each week to be sure I had something good to say about his full product line. It was an innovation typical of this shy, quiet, and warmhearted man. Once, when he was besieged by radio time salesmen, each claiming that his station's audience was the best for selling cars, Mr. Byers simply walked out to his parking garage and instructed the attendants that, as they parked each car, they were to note on a sheet of paper what station was on the radio when the driver dropped it off. In short order he completed his own highly targeted audience survey, and used the results to guide his future advertising buys.

Life now settled into the first real routine I had known since working at WRFD. I would get up each morning, dress, and be at WOSU by 9 a.m. Lunch was typically a brown bag shared with co-workers in a vacant studio. My day ended by delivering the news during *On the Way Home* and soon after I, too, was on the way home. Dinner was over by 7, and by 7:30 or so Mary and our daughter, Kathy, tucked me into bed. At 10:15 p.m. Mary would come in and wake me, I would climb back into my clothes and drive downtown to WBNS, arriving a few minutes before 11. Ted Shell completed his newscast at 11:15 and a moment later I would spin Leroy Anderson's "Forgotten Dreams," my theme for *Music 'til One*. At 1 a.m., I turned the air over to Bill Corley for *The All Night Show*, sometimes grabbed a late night snack with Bill Hamilton at Benny Klein's, and soon after headed home for the second time that day. I was usually back in bed by 2:30 a.m. and slept until 7:30 when it started all over again. Mary and I have sometimes wondered what impressions our three-year-old was left with, putting daddy to bed instead of the other way around.

An interesting feature of the tiny studio from which I broadcast was a small gray box that monitored the CBS Radio Network. By design, all feeds from the network (mostly newscasts by the mid-'60s) were scheduled on the daily log and were a regular part of WBNS broadcast day—CBS News on the hour, followed by local news and weather, then nothing more from the network until the top of the next hour. But if major news broke between the scheduled newscasts, a number would come up on the small gray box indicating 1) the importance of the breaking story (with one being lowest and six [I think] being highest); and 2) that the network would start its feed in exactly sixty-seconds. The station could then interrupt its current programming and switch to the network for the breaking news.

During my late night/early morning shift, the gray box almost never showed any number but zero. Sometimes a higher number would suddenly appear, but when I checked the network feed there was nothing there but test tone. One night I checked the network and heard the sound of a dance band. I was going to ignore it, but I was suddenly seized with an inspiration. When the music I was playing came to an end, I reminded my listeners that, in years past, the networks frequently broadcast dance bands from ballrooms around the country, but they hadn't done so in almost twenty years. Yet here, tonight (sneak in music behind my monolog), the CBS network was once again feeding dance music to its affiliated stations. There's no announcer, so I can't tell you what the band is, or where it's performing. I can't even tell you if it's live music or a recording. But ... maybe ... it's neither. Maybe it's an echo—an electronic reverberation that's been trapped somewhere in CBS control for more than two decades and is just now finding its way onto the net. Some phantom sound that may have accompanied a New Year's Eve during World War II, when young pilots and soldiers and seamen were enjoying a last, desperate stateside romance. Then the sound became imprisoned by the rush of events—Ed Murrow, blitzkrieg, London bombings. Now, with America again at war, the sound had found its way out of history and back onto the net. Maybe ... just maybe, that's what we're hearing now.

I played with the listeners for about ten minutes and then returned to regular programming. The cards and letters that followed helped me to understand how willing a nighttime radio audience was to follow its imaginations wherever I chose to lead.

One Friday night in June 1964, the gray box suddenly came to life. The numbers started low, but quickly built to six. When the network feed began, it had very much the controlled frenzy I remembered from the initial coverage of the JFK assassination. This story, too, involved a Kennedy: thirty-two-year-old U.S. Senator from Massachusetts, Ted Kennedy. He had been a passenger aboard a plane that had crashed in Minnesota. The pilot and one of Kennedy's aides, Edward Moss, had been killed. The story, still new, was seeking confirmation that Kennedy had been pulled from the wreckage by his fellow Democrat Senator, Birch Bayh, II.

Music 'til One was beginning to build an audience. Broadcast both on AM and in FM stereo, paid for by low-key, brief, and occasionally inventive commercials, and featuring the latest stereo releases that conformed to my personal criteria for late night music, the number of listeners grew until it was the second-rated program in its time slot. At the same time, my career at WOSU continued to develop, as noted earlier, until I held the second highest position at the station.

Life was very good, indeed. And an old lie was about to bring it all to an end.

DIRECTING basketball great John Havlicek in a TV spot for my advertising agency, TRIAD, after leaving broadcasting.

Once again the phone in the newsroom was ringing. This time the caller was Martha Haueisen, administrative assistant to Dr. Richard B. Hull, head of Ohio State's Telecommunications Center, the parent department of WOSU AM/FM/TV. Martha reported that a routine check of university records had failed to locate any mention of my graduation from the university, and could it be that it was filed under a different name? In an instant my career at WOSU was at an end.

When I had filled out the application for employment with WOSU I was an unemployed husband who needed work and was not willing to lose a job he had already been offered for lack of a degree. So, with a sense of shame but also with a belief in myself and my ability to do the job, degree or no, I had lied and said I was a graduate. Now, the truth would be discovered within a matter of days, if not hours. As I hung up the phone I was glad that the university insisted on contracts with all its employees. I would not be fired; my contract would simply not be renewed. And that would buy me a couple of months to find other employment.

When the truth became known, I was told by the station manager that, indeed, my contract would not be renewed, but that no one need know the reason, certainly not my co-workers. That afternoon I drafted a memo to the staff telling them precisely why I was being terminated and apologizing to them for my perfidy. I guess I had lived with one lie for so long that I wasn't about to cover it up with another.

In the short run, life continued as before. But my work for Byers on WBNS had already stirred an awareness in me that what I most enjoyed about the program was ad libbing the commercials, and that thinking my way through a sales premise—finding a beginning, providing a middle, and inventing the big close—gave me great satisfaction. I'd become aware that WTVN's baseball broadcaster, Joe Hill, had left the station and, together with Chuck Angeletti, had formed an advertising agency called Joe Hill and Associates. I'd met Joe for lunch and asked if he needed a copywriter. He said he did, but couldn't afford one at that moment, and that I should stay in touch. Now, as I put the phone down from talking with Martha, I picked it up again and called Joe.

Joe was familiar with my work for Byers and impressed that the commercials were extemporaneous. He loved the idea of my coming to work for him, but still wasn't able to add a position to his fledgling agency. I told him I would be available when the time was right. Meanwhile, I set about finding a position that would feed my family in the interim.

The new job offer, when it came, was interesting for a number of reasons. It was fulltime, but understood by all parties to be temporary. It was in radio, but it wasn't an air position. It was with WRFD and it came through Phil Sheridan, the man who had fired me previously. And I would be selling radio as a service, but not for the purpose of advertising.

A bit more radio lore may be helpful. An FM signal, called a carrier, has two additional carriers that piggyback on it. These additional carriers, called sidebands, are present whether they are used or not. One sideband, together with the main carrier, is required for FM stereo broadcasting. But that leaves the remaining sideband with nothing to do. WVKO Radio in Columbus in the mid-1960s leased one of its sidebands to Muzak as a way of delivering background music to shops, stores, offices, and restaurants that subscribed to the service. The technique was really very simple. It consisted of connecting speakers located throughout the subscriber's premises with a tuner that was capable of receiving only the sideband's frequency (that is, without the main carrier or other sideband), and then amplifying that signal for as many speakers as were necessary. The music delivered by sideband was entirely separate from the station's FM signal. It was as if two radio stations were sharing the same transmitter. WRFD was going to do the same thing with one of its sidebands, providing its own background music service called *The Sound of Magic*.

My job was to meet with business owners and office managers to persuade them to let me put a tuner and speakers in their facilities for a one month free trial. I encountered little resistance to my offer and soon had placed a number of tuners in offices throughout Columbus. Huntington National Bank had just completed a new multi-floor downtown facility to house its trust department, and because the cost of our service was based on the number of speakers installed in a facility, a sale there would represent a major source of revenue to WRFD and a major success for my fledgling sales career. But they were proving to be a difficult sell.

Typically, a business owner would "audition" our service with a tuner and a single speaker placed next to his or her desk.

But Huntington wanted a more realistic trial, and asked me to install a series of speakers above the ceiling tiles in the halls and offices of one floor of the new building. As a sales staff, I was a one-man-band, with no technical backup. But I was also fairly well versed on how the system worked, so one day I arrived with a box of speakers and a long coil of twin-lead wire, and by the end of the day, one floor of the trust department of Huntington National Bank was bathed in *The Sound of Magic*. By the end of the month, the Huntington agreed to become a subscriber and contracted for speakers to be located throughout the new building.

I had a rather different experience with Danny Deeds, owner of The Maramor restaurant. Danny routinely booked live acts for his supper clientele, and thought he might want a background service for his luncheon guests. I set up a tuner in the kitchen and a single speaker in the ceiling above the main dining room. At the end of the trial month, I couldn't get Danny to sign a contract. But I also couldn't get him to return the tuner and speaker. Weeks went by, and then months, with Danny not returning my calls or agreeing to meet with me when I showed up at the restaurant. I finally went to Phil Sheridan to discuss the problem. Phil listened quietly, then told me not to worry about it and just to continue selling. I later learned that Phil had a late lunch that day at The Maramor, at the end of which he walked into the kitchen, jerked the tuner off the wall and walked out of the restaurant with it under his arm, the speaker wires trailing behind. No one spoke a word to him.

There came a bit of irony as I was finishing up my years at WOSU. As I mentioned previously, *Music 'til One* was building a large nighttime audience, a fact not lost on WBNS management. One day I received a call from Russ Canter. Dean Lewis, whom I assumed was heir apparent to *The Early Worm*, was leaving the station for another market. Would I be interested in permanently assuming his afternoon shift? *Would* I? This was the culmination of everything I had been pointing toward since I entered broadcasting six years before: fulltime employment in a fixed time slot on the number-one-rated AM station in Columbus. It didn't get any better than this.

Which is why it was so hard to turn down.

Perhaps because of the closing door at WOSU, I had begun taking the first real inventory of my workplace strengths and weaknesses. I was a good broadcaster—under the right circumstances, maybe even very good. But those circumstances required late night listeners, not a midday audience. The station needed someone faster on his feet than I. Then, too, the times, as Bob Dylan had it, they were a–changin', and WBNS's commitment to a strong, middle-of-the-road music policy was already in question. I wasn't sure where it was headed, but any departure would put me at a disadvantage. Frank Sinatra, Nat Cole, Tony Bennett, and Gordon Jenkins were old and trusted radio colleagues; Conway Twitty, The Mommas and the Papas, and Janis Joplin were not. And this much I already knew about myself; I couldn't sell what I couldn't stand. This part of my decision proved to be prescient; not too long after I left the station, the music policy went through a number of revisions, including rock 'n roll. The station today is all-sports, all the time.

But the biggest factor in my decision not to accept the afternoon shift on WBNS was that I was excited at the prospect of becoming a copywriter.

As a kid I had played at writing even before I played at radio, and my years in broadcasting had convinced me that I was prepared to compete with other copywriters in the area. With all the misgivings that accompany the making of a potentially life-altering decision, I called Russ back and declined his offer.

I had one more on-air hurrah before I left broadcasting for good. My pal, Al Franz, from Discount Records asked to buy an hour of airtime on WRFD-FM each week to spotlight new classical recordings that arrived at his store, and he was kind enough to specify that I be the host. The station did a maximum promotional effort on the new program, but the FM audience still wasn't there, and when, after thirteen weeks, the broadcasts had not built traffic for his store, Al ended his sponsorship.

In February of 1966, I walked out of a radio studio for the last time as a member of the staff. It had been a wild and joyous ride, and there are very few memories whose outcomes I would choose to change. Joe Hill had finally found business enough to hire me as a copywriter. I joined Chuck Angeletti, art director Karl Wise, producer Johnny Metzger (who wrote "This is Ohio State 1960"), and a few others as a Joe Hill associate and began to learn the advertising trade.

A year later, Paul Myers hired me to be creative director of PAM Advertising, and there I met a future partner, Lee Ault. Now, in addition to being the agency's principal writer, I was responsible for it's total creative output, including print, radio, and TV.

In 1970, I left PAM to become vice president of Angeletti and Wise, a new agency formed by Joe Hill's former partner, together with his former art director. My role was to develop my own stable of accounts, for which I would provide creative as well as account management services. It was during this time that I met Jeff Keeler, a man who would remain my largest and most loyal client, and my closest business friend, throughout my thirty-six years in advertising. Jeff succeeded his father-in-law, Ken Fishel, as the president and CEO of The Fishel Company, a nationally deployed, underground utility construction firm self-styled "The World's Greatest—and Safest—Ditch Diggers." Jeff died about the time I was midway through this book. I had promised to let him read it; I wish mightily I were able to make that happen.

I had one move remaining, and that occurred October 1, 1972. This was the day TRIAD, Incorporated opened its doors. TRIAD is an advertising and public relations practice I co-founded with Lee Ault and Pat Reynolds (three in advertising, hence TRIAD). For the next thirty years, I was constantly, happily, and exhaustedly immersed in the marketing needs of a variety of clients. For the Ohio State Fair, I wrote the lyrics for a succession of jingles, working with many talented composers and recording groups, including The Arbors and a young Sandi Patti. I wrote and produced several performances of a live, multi-media fundraising presentation for the Columbus Symphony Orchestra that employed nine slide projectors, an original score by John Tatgenhorst (famous for his arrangement of "Hang On, Sloopy" for The Ohio State University Marching Band), a narrator, and the entire orchestra under John's direction. And I was project manager of our company's successful bid to produce the commemorative program for The American Freedom Train, 1975-76.

In the latter capacity, I traveled up and down the eastern seaboard with a layout artist and a photographer, rushing to complete an eighteen-page, four-color souvenir booklet. Included were photos of many of the priceless artifacts that were to travel aboard the train, but were still in the possession of their donors, which explains the need to travel. Despite enormous frustrations with the Freedom Train's management team that was almost childlike in its jealousies and unpredictability, we completed the task and delivered a printed program in just six sleepless weeks. Stan Bowen was the artist and Warren Motts the photographer. I provided the art direction and text. At one point, needing to enter the Library of Congress in order to photograph various documents that would travel with the train, Warren and I were denied access after passing through security, because a member of the management team who thought she should have been consulted about our visit, and wasn't, picked up the phone and pulled the plug on our entry. The next day, when appropriate attention had been paid to her backside, she approved our visit, but we had lost twenty-four precious hours.

The visit to the library was a wonder. Descending in an elevator without markings as to the number of floors, we emerged into a narrow hall and were led to a fully equipped photo studio. A few minutes later an employee wheeled in a library cart piled high with red folders whose openings were secured by flaps laced with red string tied between two red buttons. We had not been told what to expect; indeed, I'm not sure any member of the management team then knew what the library had decided to let travel aboard the train. We were told that we had an hour to complete our photography, after which our guide left. As I opened the first folder, my mouth dropped in wonder. It was an original draft of the U.S. Constitution with George Washington's hand-written notes in the margin. Each new folder offered something equally astonishing. In my hands, at one time or another, were our government's copies of such famous treaties as the Louisiana Purchase, the Gadsden Purchase, and the Oregon Compromise; various treaties with Native American tribes, the tribal leaders signing with Xs; a draft version of the Emancipation Proclamation; and Roosevelt's "Day of Infamy" address to Congress, with FDR's last minute changes written in ink.

The train and its artifacts left Wilmington, Delaware, in the spring of 1975 and spent the next year circumnavigating the

United States. My company was retained to make updates to the program from time to time, but slowly the project began to wind down. I became a member and later president of the Columbus Society of Communicating Arts. A few years later I was asked to join the Friends of WOSU, a statewide organization providing financial support and program guidance to the university's AM/FM/TV stations. I was a member from 1981 to 1988 and served as president from 1985 to 1987. You have to smile at life's ironies.

Things were changing at TRIAD. Pat Reynolds left the firm in 1976, and I bought Lee Ault's share of the company in 1986 when he decided to enter the ministry (his former partner, Paul Myers, had also entered the ministry). Thereafter, I was president of TRIAD until my retirement at the end of 2002. Today, the company is owned and managed by our son, Dave.

I was, and remain, an advertiser at heart, and I celebrate the accomplishments of the men and women who produce some of the cleverest communications the world has ever known. But I never forget that, for six wonderful years, I was privileged to be part of something special: locally owned and managed radio. Radio today is probably financially stronger than ever before, but so changed by consolidation and group ownership as to be almost unrecognizable from my years in its employment. In Columbus alone, six formerly independent stations are now collectively owned and managed by Clear Channel Communications and broadcast from the same building. Happily for me, a half century ago, local radio's needs were not beyond my youth and inexperience to satisfy. By paying little attention to income and even less to the burgeoning careers of my non-broadcast friends, I was able to experience the tremendous power of a medium that could leap hundreds of miles in a fraction of a second, reducing the distance to the few steps that separated a listener from his radio. I could even experiment with radio's oft-mentioned advantage over TV to the effect that faces and places created in your mind were never at odds with reality, never a disappointment. Not, at least, until the listener met you in person.

The pace was sometimes frantic, the money was never adequate, job security was a laugh. And I loved every minute of it. It gives me pleasure to remember that, for a little while, in a mid-size market in the middle of the last century, I was privileged to be a "monkey on a turntable."

sign off

ACKNOWLEDGEMENTS & Confessions

Ken Keller lives in Worthington, Ohio with his Ladylove of 48 years, Mary, and a cat named Truman.

Memories, I have discovered, are a slide show, while storytelling is a movie. Frozen moments of time need to be connected by narrative, and the details of that narrative may or may not live in the memory. How, then, to reconnect these almost fifty-year-old images? In most cases, the story path between events is such a straight line that it could not have happened any other way. In a very few cases, two or even three different paths are possible. In these cases, I have tried to remember myself at that age and to choose the path I am most likely to have walked. I am comfortable that every word of this narrative is as true as I can make it, except as noted in the following two paragraphs. If someone who lived a part of this journey with me remembers differently, I apologize.

My joy in storytelling is always tempered by a newsman's regard for the truth, and so a couple of modest corrections to this book are in order. The story about the "lost" interview with Aaron Copland is entirely true, but occurred outside my years in broadcasting. By 1970, the year of the interview, I was working fulltime in advertising. One of my accounts was the Columbus Symphony Orchestra, for which I also assumed the title of Publicist. The interview would be used to promote attendance at the concert, and had it gone as planned, I had arranged with Fred Calland for it to air on WOSU Radio. Fred was amused when he heard why there would be no interview.

In like manner, the recording with Yehudi Menuhin was also outside my broadcast years. Its purpose, as mentioned, was to promote the CSO's annual fund drive. For assisting me in getting the dates of these events straight, I am indebted to Alan

McCracken, who preceded the late Nat Greenberg as General Manager of the CSO, and to Susan Rosenstock, the current General Manager.

Most of the people who helped to fill in the missing spaces in my memories have been identified in the course of telling their stories. I would like to single out for special mention Charlie Pickard, who met with me on several occasions to remember the staff and facilities at both WRFD and WOSU. Charlie was also supportive of the whole idea of this book, and for that I am grateful.

I'm also grateful to my wife, Mary, who learned to live with, and even enjoy, the occasional off-the-wall questions about our early years together that I would pose. She became equally comfortable with my leaving our bed in the middle of the night to write something down that I had just remembered and did not want to chance forgetting before dawn. If you're going to travel some less-worn paths, Mary Folsom Keller is the ideal companion. Thank you, my love.

The fact that this book exists at all is due to three remarkable people. John Baskin read an early version of the manuscript and, despite its flaws, dared to recommend it to Marcy Hawley, both of Orange Frazer Press. Marcy took a more critical view of the manuscript but still agreed to publish it, insisting I turn it over to Wendy Cornett to edit. Wendy made many of the flaws go away. To each of these I am deeply grateful.

Finally, to Elizabeth Papps, who taught me to write, and more importantly, to enjoy it—a lifetime of thanks.

Sometimes, my memories were better than what actually occurred, and while grateful is too strong a word, I am glad that someone was there to set me straight. For example, I remembered that Bill Hamilton had been fired from WBNS Radio for one afternoon flying a kite from the roof of the building that housed the studios. The kite string had become wrapped around the antenna used to receive signals from the traffic plane, and so had shorted out the reception from the plane, causing a loss of income from that evening's traffic reports. He was fired on the spot by the station's chief engineer, who owned stock in the station.

"Urban legend," sniffed Bill, in his e-mail response to proofreading this part of the book. He had, indeed, flown a kite from the roof, but it had snagged on a rain gutter, not the antenna. And as far as being fired on the spot by the chief engineer, a sullen and humorless recluse whose unfailing bad temper caused Bill to refer to him as The Prince of Darkness, he only came into the building at night and so would not have been on hand to personally dispense with Bill's services. No, it was nothing more dramatic than a slow but irreversible decline in ratings, something that began before Bill's tenure and continued for the person who followed him, that proved his undoing.

Too bad. It's a good story, and I wish I could have included it in this book.